SQL Server 2005 Implementation and Maintenance

Lab Manual

JOSEPH L. JORDEN

DANDY WEYN

DAVE OWEN

WILEY

EXECUTIVE EDITOR	John Kane
DIRECTOR OF MARKETING AND SALES	Mitchell Beaton
PRODUCTION MANAGER	Micheline Frederick
PRODUCTION EDITOR	Kerry Weinstein
EDITORIAL ASSISTANT	Jennifer Lartz

To order books or for customer service, please call 1-800-CALL WILEY (225-5945).

ISBN   978-0470-11170-3
Printed in the United States of America

10 9 8 7 6 5 4 3 2 1

BRIEF CONTENTS

CONTENTS

23. Working with Replication 205

LAB 1
INTRODUCING THE COURSE

This lab contains the following exercises and activities:

Exercise 1.1   Checking for Background (Prerequisite) Knowledge

Exercise 1.1	Checking for Background (Prerequisite) Knowledge
Scenario	You need to develop or upgrade your administrative skills to include SQL Server 2005. This course presumes you have fundamental knowledge in three areas: database concepts, structured query language constructs, and Windows Server administration.
Duration	This task should take less than one hour.
Setup	This task requires no setup.
Caveats	No caveats apply to this exercise.
Procedure	In this task, you will answer background questions about concepts that apply to the prerequisites.
Equipment Used	This is a paper-and-pencil exercise.
Objective	To make certain you have the knowledge needed to successfully complete this course.
Criteria for Completion	You have completed this task when you have answered all the questions.

■ PART A: Determining Prerequisites

1. What is an RDBMS?

   _____

2. What are normalization rules?

   _____

3. What is entity integrity?

   _____

4. What is referential integrity?

   _____

5. What is OLTP?

   _____

6. What is OLAP?

   _____

7. What is a field?

   _____

8. What is a transaction?

   _____

9. What is a domain?

   _____

10. What is a user database?

   _____

11. What is unicode?

   _____

12. What is a select query?

   _____

13. What is a join condition?

   _____

14. What is a calculated column?

   _____

15. What does the SELECT statement return?

   _____

16. What is a self-join?

_____

17. What is DDL?

_____

18. What is UPDATE

_____

19. What is parameterization?

_____

20. What is a search argument?

_____

21. What is an SPN?

_____

22. What is Windows Management Instrumentation?

_____

23. What is a domain?

_____

24. In Group Policy, you may set a password policy to Password must meet complexity requirements. What are these requirements?

_____

25. When you delete a user and then recreate the same user, what happens?

_____

26. What are the six default logs in Event Viewer for a domain controller?

_____

27. In System Monitor, what Performance Object/Counter will report the available free space on a specific hard drive?

_____

28. What utility permits you to change computer passwords?

_____

29. What is a stand-alone server?

_____

30. You checked the Log On property of MSSQLSERVER from the Administrative Tools/Services menu and discover it is set to Log on as: Local System Account. Can remote users access this instance of SQL Server? Can local users access this instance of SQL Server?

_____

LAB 2
INSTALLING SQL SERVER 2005·

This lab contains the following exercises and activities:

Exercise 2.1   Installing SQL Server 2005 Manually

Exercise 2.2   Installilng a Second Instance

Exercise 2.1	Installing SQL Server 2005 Manually
Scenario	You are the database administrator (DBA) for a midsize company with offices in various cities throughout the United States and Canada. The company has decided to use SQL Server 2005 for data storage and retrieval, and you have been asked to install the software and get it running.
	As an experienced DBA, you understand the importance of installing the software right the first time, because if you install SQL Server incorrectly or on the wrong hardware, it will work slowly or not at all. Therefore, you have decided to verify the prerequisites and then install the software.
Duration	This task should take less than one hour.
Setup	This task requires little setup. All you need is access to a copy of SQL Server 2005 Enterprise Edition or Developer Edition and a computer that meets the requirements to run it.
Caveats	SQL Server 2005 runs better on faster hardware. Remember that the minimum requirements listed later in this task are just that, minimum. If you have access to a faster machine with more random access memory (RAM), use it.
Procedure	In this task, you will verify that your computer meets the requirements for running SQL Server 2005 and then install the default instance.

Equipment Used	Although several editions of SQL Server 2005 exist, you will be working with the Enterprise Edition in this book because it has the widest range of available features. You can download a 180-day trial copy of Enterprise Edition from the Microsoft website (www.microsoft.com/sql) for use in your home training environment. You will also need access to a machine that meets the prerequisites for Enterprise Edition.
Objective	To make certain your server meets the requirements for installing SQL Server 2005. Table 2-1 lists the prerequisites for installing the Standard and Developer Editions.
Criteria for Completion	You have completed this task when you have a running instance of SQL Server 2005 installed on your system.

■ PART A: Determining Prerequisites

1. Do you have a 32-bit, a 64-bit, or multiple CPUs?

_____

2. How much memory do you have?

_____

3. Do you have a DVD drive?

_____

4. How much hard drive space is available?

_____

5. What operating system do you have?

_____

6. Check Table 2-1. Do these answers meet the minimum requirements for SQL Server 2005?

_____

Table 2-1
Developer/Standard Edition Requirements

Component	32-bit	x64	Itanium
Processor	600 MHz Pentium III–compatible or faster processor; 1 GHz or faster processor recommended	1 GHz AMD Opteron, AMD Athlon 64, Intel Xeon with Intel EM64T support, Intel Pentium IV with EM64T support processor	1 GHz Itanium or faster processor
Memory	512 MB of RAM or more; 1 GB or more recommended	512 MB of RAM or more; 1 GB or more recommended	512 MB of RAM or more; 1 GB or more recommended
Disk drive	CD or DVD drive	CD or DVD drive	CD or DVD drive
Hard disk space	Approximately 350 MB of available hard disk space for the recommended installation with approximately 425 MB of additional space for SQL Server BOL, SQL Server Mobile BOL, and sample databases	Approximately 350 MB of available hard disk space for the recommended installation with approximately 425 MB of additional space for SQL Server BOL, SQL Server Mobile BOL, and sample databases	Approximately 350 MB of available hard disk space for the recommended installation with approximately 425 MB of additional space for SQL Server BOL, SQL Server Mobile BOL, and sample databases
Operating system	Microsoft Windows 2000 Server with SP4 or newer; Windows 2000 Professional Edition with SP4 or newer; Windows XP with SP2 or newer; Vista; Windows Server 2003 Enterprise Edition, Standard Edition, or Datacenter Edition with SP1 or newer; Windows Small Business Server 2003 with SP1 or newer	Microsoft Windows Server 2003 Standard x64 Edition, Enterprise x64 Edition, or Datacenter x64 Edition with SP1 or newer; Windows XP Professional x64 Edition or newer; Vista	Microsoft Windows Server 2003 Enterprise Edition or Datacenter Edition for Itanium-based systems with SP1 or newer

■ PART B: Installing SQL Server 2005

1. You need to create a service account, so create a user account named SqlServer, and make it a member of the Administrators local group. You can perform this task by using one of these tools:
   - On a Windows member server or on Windows XP, use Computer Management.
   - On a Windows domain controller, use Active Directory Users and Computers.

NOTE	*In a production environment you should make the service account owner a user with the necessary permissions and named just like any other user so hackers can't determine the account owner by inspection.*

2. Insert the SQL Server CD, and wait for the automenu to open.

3. Under Install, choose Server Components, tools, Books Online, and samples.

4. You will then be asked to read and agree with the end user license agreement (EULA); check the box to agree, and then click Next.

5. If your machine does not have all the prerequisite software installed, the setup will install them for you at this time. Click Install if you are asked to do so. When complete, click Next.

6. Next you will see a screen telling you that the setup is inspecting your system's configuration again, and then the welcome screen appears. Click Next to continue.

7. Another, more in-depth system configuration screen appears letting you know whether any configuration settings will prevent SQL Server from being installed. You need to repair errors (marked with a red icon) before you can continue. You can optionally repair warnings (marked with a yellow icon), although they will not prevent SQL Server from installing. Once you have made any needed changes, click Next.

8. After a few configuration setting screens, you will be asked for your product key. Enter it, and click Next.

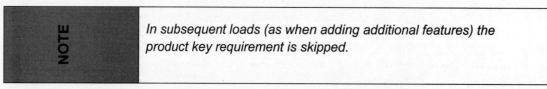

NOTE   *In subsequent loads (as when adding additional features) the product key requirement is skipped.*

9. On the next screen, you need to select the components you want to install. Check the boxes next to the SQL Server Database Services option and the Workstation Components, Books Online, and Development Tools option.

10. Click the Advanced button to view the advanced options for the setup.

11. Expand Documentation, Samples, and Sample Databases. Then click the button next to Sample Databases, select Entire Feature Will Be Installed on Local Hard Drive, and then click Next. This will install the AdventureWorks database that you will be using later in this Lab Manual.

12. On the Instance Name screen, choose Default Instance, and click Next.

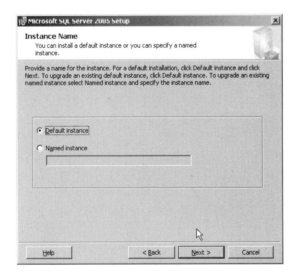

13. On the next screen, enter the account information for the service account that you created in Step 1. You will be using the same account for each service. When finished, click Next.

14. On the Authentication Mode screen, select Mixed Mode, enter the password "Pa$$w0rd" for the sa account, and click Next.

15. Select the Latin1_General collation designator on the next screen, and click Next.

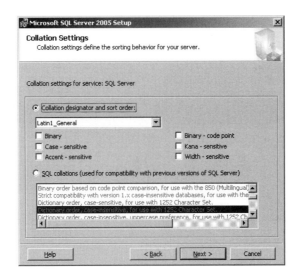

16. On the following screen, you can select to send error and feature usage information directly to Microsoft. You will not be enabling this function here. So, leave the defaults and click Next.

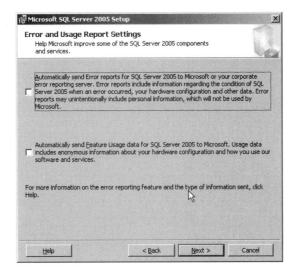

17. On the Ready to Install screen, review your settings, and then click Install.

18. The setup progress indicator appears during the install process. When the setup is finished (which may take a while), click Next.

19. The final screen gives you an installation report, letting you know whether any errors occurred and reminding you of any post-installation steps to take. Click Finish to complete your install.

20. Reboot your system if requested to do so.

■ PART C: Verifying Results

1. Click Start.
2. Click All Programs.
3. Click Microsoft SQL Server 2005.
4. Click Configuration Tools.
5. Click SQL Server Configuration Manager.

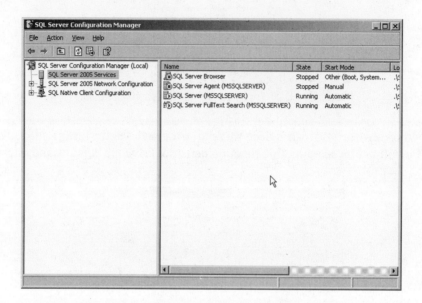

6. Select SQL Server 2005 Services, and check the icons. If the icon next to SQL Server (MSSQLServer) service is green, then your installation is a success.

Exercise 2.2	Installing a Second Instance
Scenario	You are the database administrator (DBA) for a midsize company with offices in various cities throughout the United States and Canada. You know you need an instance of SQL Server 2005 for testing new service packs, new database schemas, and the like, but your company does not have the budget for new hardware at this time. The only way for you to have a test copy of SQL Server is to install a named instance.
Duration	This task should take less than one hour.
Setup	Again, all you need for this task is the machine you used in Exercise 2.1 and the same copy of SQL Server 2005 you used in Exercise 2.1.
Caveat	This task doesn't have any caveats.
Procedure	In this task, you will install a second instance of SQL Server on the same machine you used in Exercise 2.1.

Equipment Used	All you need for this task is the machine you used in Exercise 2.1 and the same copy of SQL Server 2005 you used in Exercise 2.1.
Objective	To create a second instance of SQL Server on the same machine as the default instance.
Criteria for Completion	Check SQL Server Configuration Manager to see whether your services are running for the second instance.

■ PART A: Installing the Second Instance

1. Insert the SQL Server CD, and wait for the automenu to open.
2. Under Install, choose Server Components, tools, Books Online, and samples.
3. You will then be asked to read and agree with the end user license agreement (EULA); check the box to agree, and click Next.
4. If your machine does not have all the prerequisite software installed, the setup will install them for you at this time. Click Install if you are asked to do so. When complete, click Next.
5. Next you will see a screen telling you the setup is inspecting your system's configuration again, and then the welcome screen appears. Click Next to continue.
6. Another, more in-depth system configuration screen appears letting you know whether any configuration settings will prevent SQL Server from being installed. You need to repair errors (marked with a red icon) before you can continue. You can optionally repair warnings (marked with a yellow icon), although they will not prevent SQL Server from installing. Once you have made any needed changes, click Next.
7. After a few configuration setting screens, you will be asked for your registration information. Enter it, and click Next.
8. On the next screen, you need to select the components you want to install. Check the box next to SQL Server Database Services, and click Next.
9. On the Instance Name screen, choose Named Instance, and in the text box enter Second. Then click Next.

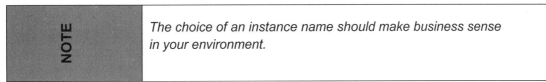

NOTE	*The choice of an instance name should make business sense in your environment.*

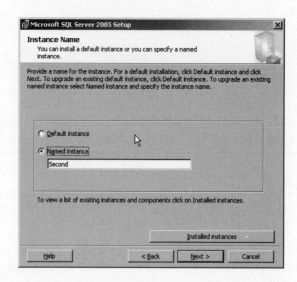

10. On the next screen, enter the account information for the service account you created in Step 1 of Exercise 2.1. You will be using the same account for each service. When finished, click Next.

11. On the Authentication Mode screen, select Mixed Mode, enter the password, "Pa$$w0rd" for the sa account, and click Next.

12. Select the Latin1_General collation designator on the next screen, and click Next.

13. On the following screen, you can select to send error and feature usage information directly to Microsoft. You will not be enabling this function here. So, leave the defaults, and click Next.

14. On the Ready to Install screen, you can review your settings, and then click Install.

15. The setup progress appears during the install process. When the setup is finished (which may take several minutes), click Next.

16. The final screen gives you an installation report, letting you know whether any errors occurred and reminding you of any post-installation steps to take. Click Finish to complete your install.

17. Reboot your system if requested to do so.

■ PART B: Verifying Results

1. Click Start.
2. Click All Programs.
3. Click Microsoft SQL Server 2005.
4. Click Configuration Tools.
5. Click SQL Server Configuration Manager.

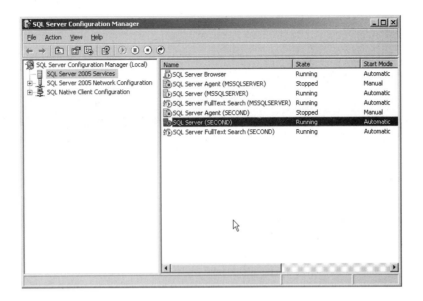

6. Select SQL Server 2005 Services, and check the icons. If the icon next to SQL Server (MSSQLServer) service is green for your new instance, then your installation is a success. If it is not green, refer to the last section of Lesson 2 of your text "Troubleshooting the Installation" for guidance.

LAB 3
NAVIGATING SQL SERVER

This lab contains the following exercises and activities:

Exercise 3.1   Locating Information by Using SQL Server 2005 Utilities

Exercise 3.1	Locating Information by Using SQL Server 2005 Utilities
Scenario	You are new to SQL Server 2005. You were hired as a trainee to be part of a new group providing support for a future installation of SQL Server 2005 at your new company. While getting ready for the new installation, architects are designing the databases, programmers are preparing code, and you are being given time to explore the RDBMS, the client tools, and the business requirements in preparation for the launch.
Duration	This task should take less than one hour.
Setup	This task requires little setup. All you need is access to a computer with SQL Server 2005 Enterprise Edition already loaded on it. You installed SQL Server 2005 in Exercise 2.1.
Caveats	This task doesn't have any caveats.
Procedure	In this task, you will verify that your computer meets the requirements for running SQL Server 2005, and then install the default instance.
Equipment Used	Although several editions of SQL Server 2005 exist, you will be working with the Enterprise Edition in this book because it has the widest range of available features. Use the computer on which you loaded SQL Server 2005 in Exercise 2.1.
Objective	To practice using the four main utilities provided with SQL Server 2005.
Criteria for Completion	You have completed this task when you have answered all of the questions correctly.

■ PART A: Locating Information

1. What is the identity seed property for the FirstName column of the Person.Contact table in the AdventureWorks database?

    _____

2. How many different DBCC (Transact-SQL) statements does Microsoft supply with SQL Server 2005?

    _____

3. How do you enable xp_cmdshell using the Surface Area Configuration utility?

    _____

4. How many protocols are supplied by Microsoft by default for the SQL Server service?

    _____

5. Where do you add a new user to the SQLAgentOperatorRole?

    _____

6. What does the pipe symbol (|) mean in Transact-SQL?

    _____

7. What is your current configuration for remote connections?

    _____

8. How many database services are currently started? (Do not use Administrative Tools.)

    _____

9. Where do you find the User Mapping configuration page?

    _____

10. What is stored in the Resource hidden database?

    _____

11. What is the easiest way to add a new user to the SysAdmin role?

    _____

12. How can you easily get a list of all blocking transactions for the AdventureWorks database?

    _____

13. What are the two keys defined for the Person.Address table in the AdventureWorks database?

    _____

14. What is the Microsoft Document Explorer and how to you install it?

    _____

15. Using Management Studio, what datatype is returned when you use the Difference function?

_____

16. Using Management Studio, what is the maximum length in bytes of the parameter you may pass to the sp_help system stored procedure?

_____

LAB 4
WORKING WITH DATATYPES

This lab contains the following exercises and activities:

Exercise 4.1   Creating a Datatype by Using SSMS Object Explorer

Exercise 4.1	Creating a Datatype by Using SSMS Object Explorer
Scenario	You have been tasked by your company to support the Enterprise planners and the developers by creating needed objects in SQL Server 2005. The Enterprise planners have completed their IDEF(0), IDEF(1X), and affinity analysis; the developers are designing the database table layouts (schema). Your job is to create needed objects. Your first task is to create a custom data type.
Duration	This task should take less than fifteen minutes.
Setup	This task requires little setup. All you need is access to a copy of SQL Server 2005 Enterprise Edition and a computer that meets the requirements to run it.
Caveats	This task has no caveats.
Procedure	Use SQL Server Management Studio's Object Explore and included Query Editor to complete these tasks.
Equipment Used	Although several editions of SQL Server 2005 exist, you will be working with the Enterprise Edition in this book because it has the widest range of available features. You can download a 180-day trial copy of Enterprise Edition from the Microsoft website (www.microsoft.com/sql). You will also need access to a machine that meets the prerequisites for Enterprise Edition.
Objective	To understand two methods of creating alias datatypes for use in table definitions and other development tasks.
Criteria for Completion	You have completed this task when you check Object Explorer and find your new definitions recorded in system tables.

■ PART A: Creating an Alias Datatype by Using the Object Explorer

1. Click Start, point to All Programs, point to Microsoft SQL Server 2005, and then click SQL Server Management Studio. Connect to your default instance by assuring Database Engine, *<YourServerName>*, and windows authentication are listed. Click Connect.

2. If Object Explorer is not visible, click Object Explore on the View menu.

3. In Object Explorer, expand Databases, AdventureWorks, Programmability, and Types.

4. Right-click Types, and then click New User-Defined Data Type...

5. Enter the following information:
    Schema: dbo
    Name: CountryCode
    Data type: Char
    Length: 2
    Allow NULLs: Selected

■ PART B: Creating an Alias Dataype by Using Transact-SQL Code

1. In SQL Server Management Studio, click the New Query button on the toolbar.

2. In the new, blank query window, type the following Transact-SQL code:

```
USE AdventureWorks

CREATE TYPE dbo.EmailAddress

FROM varchar(6)

NULL;
```

3. Click the Execute button on the toolbar or Press F5.

■ PART C: Verifying Results

1. Right-click the User-defined Data Types folder in Object Explore and then click Refresh.

2. Verify that CountryCode and EmailAddress have both been added to the database.

LAB 5
WORKING WITH DATABASES

This lab contains the following exercises and activities:

Exercise 5.1   Creating a Database

Exercise 5.2   Selecting and Setting a Recovery Model

Exercise 5.1	Creating a Database
Scenario	You are the DBA for a midsize company with offices in various cities throughout the United States and Canada. You have just installed a new instance of SQL Server, and now you need to create a database to hold data for your sales department.
Duration	This task should take approximately 30 minutes.
Setup	All you need for this task is access to the machine that you installed SQL Server 2005 on in Exercise 2.1.
Caveats	This task doesn't have any caveats.
Procedure	In this task, you will create a database that will hold data for the sales department. You will use this database in later tasks for storing other database objects as well.
Equipment Used	All you need for this task is access to the machine you installed SQL Server 2005 on in Exercise 2.1.
Objective	To decide where to put the data and log files. Use these guidelines: • Data and log files should be on separate physical drives so that, in case of a disaster, you have a better chance of recovering all data.

	• Transaction logs are best placed on a RAID-1 array because this has the fastest sequential write speed together with redundancy. • Data files are best placed on a RAID-5 array because they have faster read speed than other RAID-arrays together with redundancy. • If you have access to a RAID-10 array, you can place data and log files on it because it has all the advantages of RAID-1 and RAID-0.
Criteria for Completion	You have completed this task when you have a database named Sales that you can see in SQL Server Management Studio.

■ PART A: Calculating the Storage Requirements

1. Calculate the space used by a single row of the table.
    - To do this, add the storage requirements for each datatype in the table.
    - Add the null bitmap using this formula: null_bitmap = 2 + ((number of columns + 7) /8).
    - Calculate the space required for variable length columns using this formula: variable_datasize = 2 + (num_variable_columns X 2) + max_varchar_size.
    - Calculate the total row size using this formula: Row_Size = Fixed_Data_Size + Variable_Data_Size + Null_Bitmap + Row_Header. The row header is always 4 bytes.

2. Calculate the number of rows that will fit on one page. Each page is 8,192 bytes with a header, so each page holds 8,096 bytes of data. Therefore, calculate the number of rows using this formula: 8096 ÷ (RowSize + 2).

3. Estimate the number of rows the table will hold. No formula exists to calculate this; you just need to have a good understanding of your data and user community.

4. Calculate the total number of pages that will be required to hold these rows. Use this formula: Total Number of Pages = Number of Rows in Table / Number of Rows Per Page.

Question 1	*Why bother with calculations? You can always allocate more disk storage, right?*

■ PART B: Creating a Database Named Sales

1. Start SQL Server Management Studio.
2. Connect to your default instance of SQL Server.
3. Expand your Databases folder.
4. Right-click either the Databases folder in the console tree or the white space in the right pane, and choose New Database from the context menu.
5. You should now see the General tab of the Database properties sheet. Enter the database name Sales, and leave the owner as <default>.
6. In the Database files grid, in the Logical Name column, change the name of the Sales file to Sales_Data. Use the default location for the file, and make sure the initial size is 3.

7. Click the ellipsis button (the one with three periods) in the Autogrowth column for the Sales_Data file. In the dialog box that opens, check the Restricted File Growth radio button, and restrict the filegrowth to 20 MB.

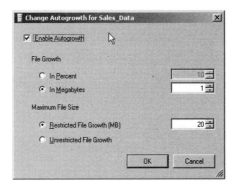

8. To add a secondary data file, click the Add button, and change the logical name of the new file to Sales_Data2. Here, too, use the default location for the file, and make sure the initial size is 3.

9. Restrict the filegrowth to a maximum of 20 MB for Sales_Data2 by clicking the ellipsis button in the Autogrowth column.

10. Leave all of the defaults for the Sales_Log file.

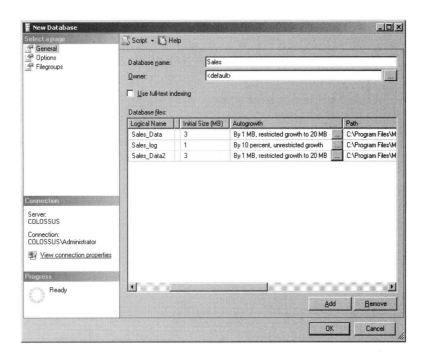

11. Click OK when you are finished. You should now have a new Sales database.

■ PART C: Verifying Results

1. In the Object Browser, click databases.
2. Press F5 or right-click database and choose refresh.
3. Verify that your new database named Sales now appears.

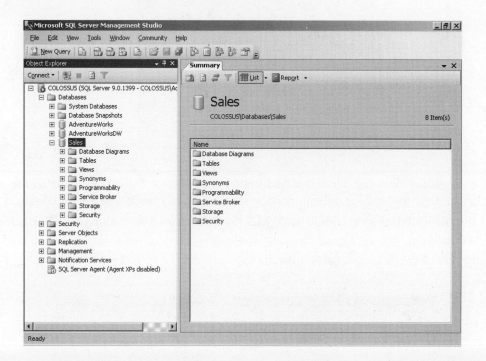

Exercise 5.2	Selecting and Setting a Recovery Model
Scenario	You have created a new database on your SQL Server, and you need to make sure it is being backed up as quickly and efficiently as possible. You know that to ensure this, you need to configure the database to use the correct recovery model, so you decide to set the recovery model for the new database.
Duration	This task should take approximately 15 minutes.
Setup	For this task, you need access to the machine you installed SQL Server 2005 on in Exercise 2.1 and the AdventureWorks database installed with the sample data.
Caveat	This task doesn't have any caveats.
Procedure	In this task, you will configure the AdventureWorks database to use the Full recovery model.
Equipment Used	For this task, you need access to the machine you installed SQL Server 2005 on in Exercise 2.1 and the AdventureWorks database installed with the sample data.

Objective	To set the recovery model for the AdventureWorks database.
Criteria for Completion	This task is complete when the AdventureWorks database is configured to use the Full recovery model as outlined in the details of this task.

■ PART A: Setting the Recovery Model

1. Open SQL Server Management Studio, and in Object Explorer, expand Databases under your server.
2. Right-click AdventureWorks, and click Properties.
3. On the Options page, select Full from the Recovery Model drop-down list.

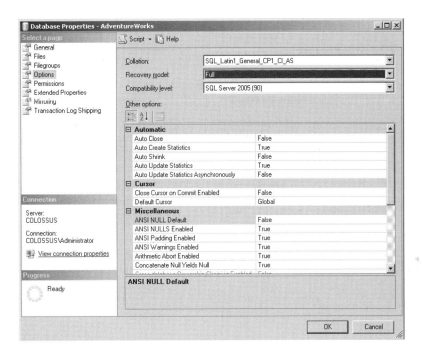

4. Click OK to configure the model.

Question 2	*Which configuration consumes the most log space?*

■ PART B: Verifying Results

1. Open Management Studio.
2. Open your Query Editor.
3. Run this code:

```
SELECT DATABASEPROPERTYEX('AdventureWorks', 'Recovery')
```

LAB 6
WORKING WITH TABLES

This lab contains the following exercises and activities:

Exercise 6.1   Designing and Creating Tables

Exercise 6.1	Designing and Creating Tables
Scenario	You have just created a database for your sales department, and now you need to create some tables to hold customer, product, and order data.
Duration	This task should take approximately 30 minutes.
Setup	All you need for this task is access to the machine you installed SQL Server 2005 on in Exercise 2.1 and the Sales database you created in Exercise 5.1.
Caveats	Remember that this is just an exercise. In the real world, you would probably have multiple tables for each of these categories. For example, you would have an OrderHeader table and an Order Details table to store multiple line items for a single order. You are creating a single table for each category in this task only for the sake of simplicity.
Procedure	In this task, you will create three tables in your Sales database: • A Products table • A Customers table • An Orders table
Equipment Used	All you need for this task is access to the machine you installed SQL Server 2005 on in Exercise 2.1 and the Sales database you created in Exercise 5.1.

Objective	To create three tables based on the criteria shown in Table 6-1, Table 6-2, and Table 6-3.
Criteria for Completion	You have completed this task when you have the Products, Customers, and Orders tables in your database with the columns defined in the exercise.

Table 6-1

Products Table Attributes

Field Name	Datatype	Contains
ProdID	Int, Identity	A unique ID number for each product that can be referenced in other tables to avoid data duplication
Description	Nvarchar(100)	A brief text description of the product
InStock	Int	The amount of product in stock

Table 6-2

Customers Table Attributes

Field Name	Datatype	Contains
CustID	Int, Identity	A unique number for each customer that can be referenced in other tables
Fname	Nvarchar(20)	The customer's first name
Lname	Nvarchar(20)	The customer's last name
Address	Nvarchar(50)	The customer's street address
City	Nvarchar(20)	The city where the customer lives
State	Nchar(2)	The state where the customer lives
Zip	Nchar(5)	The customer's zip code
Phone	Nchar(10)	The customer's phone number without hyphens or parentheses (to save space, those will be displayed but not stored)

Table 6-3
Orders Table Attributes

Field Name	Datatype	Contains
CustID	Int	References the customer number stored in the Customers table so you don't need to duplicate the customer information for each order placed
ProdID	Int	References the Products table so you don't need to duplicate product information
Qty	Int	The amount of product sold for an order
OrdDate	Smalldatetime	The date and time the order was placed

■ PART A: Creating the Products Table

1. Open SQL Server Management Studio. In Object Explorer, expand your server, and expand Databases and then Sales.

2. Right-click the Tables icon, and select New Table to open the table designer.

3. In the first row, under Column Name, enter ProdID.

4. Just to the right of that, under Data Type, select Int.

5. Make certain Allow Nulls isn't checked. The field can be completely void of data if this option is checked, and you don't want that here.

6. In the bottom half of the screen, under Column Properties, in the Table Designer section, expand Identity Specification, and change (Is Identity) to Yes.

7. Just under ProdID, in the second row under Column Name, enter Description.

8. Just to the right of that, under Data Type, enter nvarchar(100).

9. Make certain Allow Nulls is cleared.

10. Under Column Name in the third row, enter InStock.

11. Under Data Type, select Int.

12. Uncheck Allow Nulls.

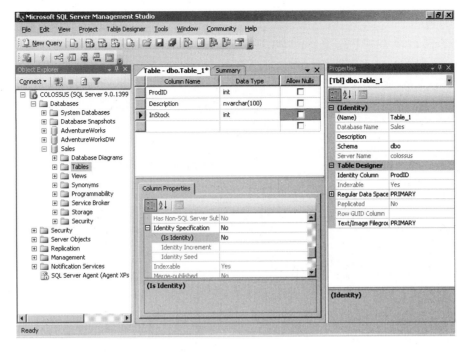

13. Click the Save button on the left side of the toolbar (it looks like a floppy disk).

14. In the Choose Name box that opens, enter Products, and then click OK.

15. Close the table designer by clicking the X in the upper-right corner of the window.

■ PART B: Creating the Customers Table

1. Right-click the Tables icon, and select New Table to open the table designer.

2. In the first row, under Column Name, enter CustID.

3. Under Data Type, select Int.

4. Make certain Allow Nulls isn't checked.

5. Under Column Properties, in the Table Designer section, expand Identity Specification, and change (Is Identity) to Yes.

6. Just under CustID, in the second row under Column Name, enter Fname.

7. Just to the right of that, under Data Type, enter nvarchar(20).

8. Make certain Allow Nulls is unchecked.

9. Using the parameters displayed earlier, fill in the information for the remaining columns. Don't allow nulls in any of the fields.

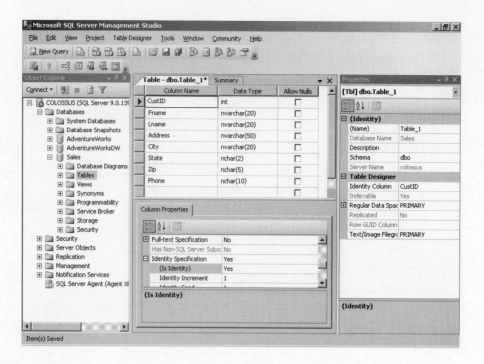

10. Click the Save button.

11. In the Choose Name box that opens, enter Customers, and then click OK.

12. Close the table designer.

■ PART C: Creating the Orders Table

1. Right-click the Tables icon, and select New Table to open the table designer.

2. In the first row, under Column Name, enter CustID.

3. Under Data Type, select Int.

4. Make certain Allow Nulls isn't checked.

5. This won't be an identity column like it was in the Customers table, so don't make any changes to the Identity Specification settings.

6. Just under CustID, in the second row under Column Name, enter ProdID with a datatype of int. Don't change the Identity Specification settings. Don't allow null values.

7. Just below ProdID, create a field named Qty with a datatype of int that doesn't allow nulls.

8. Create a column named OrdDate with a datatype of smalldatetime. Don't allow null values.

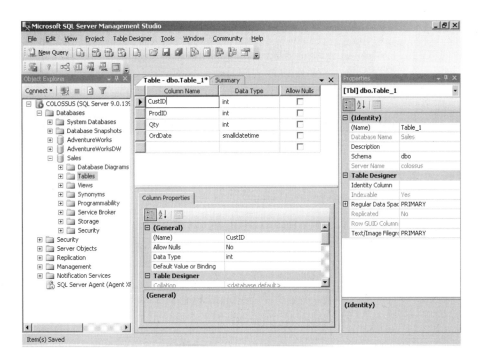

9. Click the Save button.

10. In the Choose Name box that opens, enter Orders, and then click OK.

11. Close the table designer.

■ PART D: Verifying Results

1. Expand your Sales database in SQL Server Management Studio, and then expand Tables; you should see all three tables.

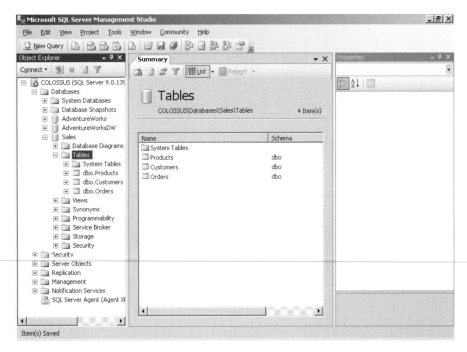

LAB 7
WORKING WITH INDEXES

This lab contains the following exercises and activities:

Exercise 7.1   Designing and Creating a Clustered Index

Exercise 7.2   Designing and Creating a Nonclustered Index

Exercise 7.3   Designing and Creating a Full-Text Index

Exercise 7.1	Designing and Creating a Clustered Index
Scenario	You have created a database for your sales department with a table that contains customer information. Your sales representatives have started complaining about slow access times. You know that the sales representatives look up customers based on their zip codes quite often, so you decide to create a clustered index on the zip column of the Customers table to improve data access times.
Duration	This task should take approximately 15 minutes.
Setup	For this task, you need access to the machine you installed SQL Server 2005 on in Exercise 2.1, the Sales database you created in Exercise 5.1, and the Customers tables you created in Exercise 6.1.
Caveat	Because this is just a test system and Customers is a small table with little data, you will not see a significant improvement in data access time.
Procedure	In this task, you will create a clustered index on the Customers table based on the Zip column.

Equipment Used	For this task, you need access to the machine you installed SQL Server 2005 on in Exercise 2.1, the Sales database you created in Exercise 5.1, and the Customers table you created in Exercise 6.1.
Objective	To create a new idx_cl_Zip clustered index.
Criteria for Completion	This task is complete when you have a clustered index on the Zip column of the Customers table in the Sales database.

■ PART A: Designing and Creating a Clustered Index

1. Open SQL Server Management Studio, and connect using Windows Authentication.
2. In Object Explorer, expand your server, and then expand Databases, Sales, Tables, and dbo.Customers.
3. Right-click Indexes, and select New Index.
4. In the Index name box, enter idx_cl_Zip.
5. Select Clustered for the index type.
6. Click the Add button next to the Index Key Columns grid.
7. Check the box next to the Zip column.

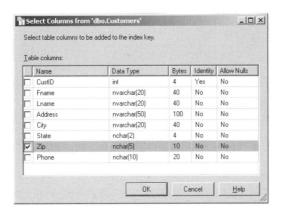

8. Click OK to return to the New Index dialog box.

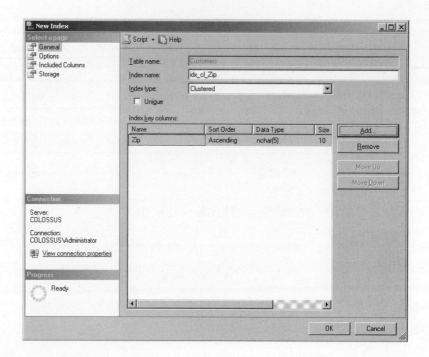

9. Click OK to create the index.

Question 1	What happens when you try to create a second clustered index on a table? Try it on Customers.Lname.

■ PART B: Verifying Results

1. Expand Databases, Sales, Tables, dbo.Customers, Indexes, and you should see the idx_cl_Zip index listed.

Exercise 7.2	Designing and Creating a Nonclustered Index
Scenario	You have created a database for your sales department with a table that contains customer information. You want to make sure data access is as fast as possible. After some investigation, you have discovered that your sales representatives consistently search for customer information by searching for a last name. Because they search only for a single record at a time, you decide to create a nonclustered index on the Lname column of the Customers table to improve data access times.
Duration	This task should take approximately 15 minutes.
Setup	For this task, you need access to the machine you installed SQL Server 2005 on in Exercise 2.1, the Sales database you created in Exercise 5.1, and the Customers table you created in Exercise 6.1.

Caveat	Because this is just a test system and Customers is a small table with little data, you will not see a significant improvement in data access time.
Procedure	In this task, you will create a nonclustered index on the Customers table based on the Lname column.
Equipment Used	For this task, you need access to the machine you installed SQL Server 2005 on in Exercise 2.1, the Sales database you created in Exercise 5.1, and the Customers table you created in Exercise 6.1.
Objective	To create a new idx_ncl_Lname nonclustered index.
Criteria for Completion	This task is complete when you have a nonclustered index on the Lname column of the Customers table in the Sales database.

■ PART A: Designing and Creating a Nonclustered Index

1. Open SQL Server Management Studio, and connect using Windows Authentication.
2. In Object Explorer, expand your server, and then expand Databases, Sales, Tables, dbo.Customers.
3. Right-click Indexes, and select New Index.
4. In the Index Name box, enter idx_ncl_Lname.
5. Select Nonclustered for the index type.
6. Click the Add button next to the Index Key Columns grid.
7. Check the box next to the Lname column.

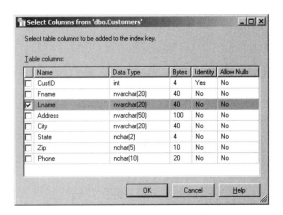

8. Click OK to return to the New Index dialog box.

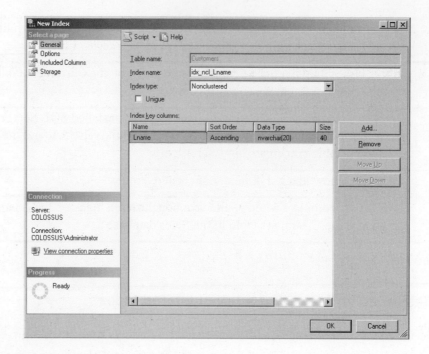

9. Click OK to create the index.

Question 2	What happens when you try to create a second nonclustered index on a table? Try it on Customers.Fname.

■ PART B: Verifying Results

1. Expand Databases, Sales, Tables, dbo.Customers, Indexes, and you should see the idx_ncl_Lname index listed.

Exercise 7.3	Designing and Creating a Full-Text Index
Scenario	One of the databases that your company has been using for some time contains a table that stores large documents. Your users have been using standard SELECT statements to access the documents in this table, but that method is proving too slow now that the table is starting to grow. You want to make sure users can query the table and get results as quickly and easily as possible, so you decide to create a full-text index on the table.
Duration	This task should take approximately 20 minutes.
Setup	For this task, you need access to the machine you installed SQL Server 2005 on in Exercise 2.1 and the AdventureWorks database that is installed with the sample data.
Caveats	This task doesn't have any caveats.

Procedure	In this task, you will create a full-text catalog and index on the Production.Document table of the AdventureWorks database.
Equipment Used	For this task, you need access to the machine you installed SQL Server 2005 on in Exercise 2.1 and the AdventureWorks database that is installed with the sample data.
Objective	To create a new full-text catalog and index on the Production.Document table.
Criteria for Completion	This task is complete when you have a full-text index on the Production.Document table of the AdventureWorks database.

■ PART A: Designing and Creating a Full-Text Index

1. Open SQL Server Management Studio, and in Object Explorer, expand Databases, AdventureWorks, and Tables.

2. Right-click Production.Document, move to Full-Text Index, and then click Define Full-Text Index.

3. On the first screen of the Full-Text Indexing Wizard, click Next.

4. Each table on which you create a full-text index must already have a unique index (primary key) associated with it for the FullText Search service to work. In this instance, select the default PK_Document_DocumentID index, and click Next.

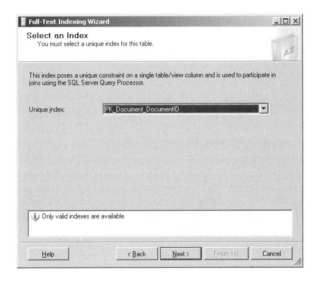

5. On the next screen, you are asked which column you want to full-text index. Document- Summary is the only nvarchar(max) column in the table, so it is the best candidate; select the box next to it, and click Next.

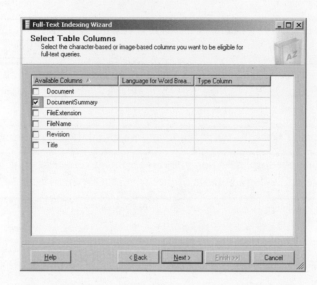

6. On the next screen, you are asked when you want changes to the full-text index applied:

   - Automatically means the full-text index is updated with every change made to the table. This is the fastest, least-hassle way to keep full-text indexes up-to-date, but it can tax the server because it means the changes to the table and index take place all at once.

   - Manually means changes to the underlying data are maintained, but you will have to schedule index population yourself. This is a slightly slower way to update the index, but it is not as taxing on the server because changes to the data are maintained but the index is not updated immediately.

   - Do Not Track Changes means changes to the underlying data are not tracked. This is the least taxing and slowest way to update the full-text index. Changes are not maintained, so when the index is updated, the FullText Search service must read the entire table for changes before updating the index.

7. Choose Automatically, and click Next.

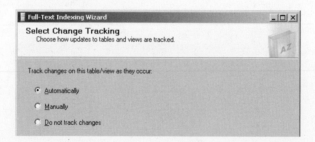

8. The next screen asks you to select a catalog. You'll need to create one here, because you don't have any available. In the Name field, enter AdventureWorks Catalog. You can also select a filegroup to place the catalog on; leave this as default, and click Next.

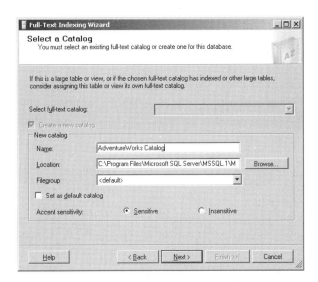

9. On the next screen, you are asked to create a schedule for automatically repopulating the full-text index. If your data is frequently updated, you will want to do this more often, maybe once a day. If it is read more often than it is changed, you should repopulate less frequently. You can schedule population for a single table or an entire catalog at a time. Here, you will set repopulation to happen just once for the entire catalog by clicking the New Catalog Schedule button.

10. On the New Schedule Properties screen, enter Populate AdventureWorks, and click OK.

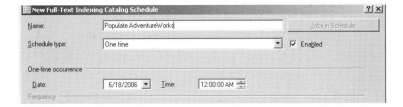

11. When you are taken back to the Full-Text Indexing Wizard, click Next.

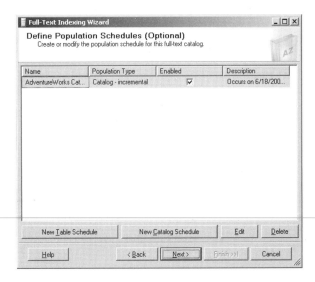

12. On the final screen of the wizard, you are given a summary of the choices you have made. Click Finish to create the index.

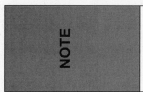

NOTE	If you work for ABC Corporation, it does no good to include ABC and words like "the" and "and" and "it" as each will have too many hits to be useful. Include such terms in the Noise Words file to exclude them.

■ PART B: Verifying Results

1. To see your new catalog and index, in Object Explorer expand AdventureWorks, Storage, Full Text Catalogs.
2. Double-click the AdventureWorks catalog to open its properties.

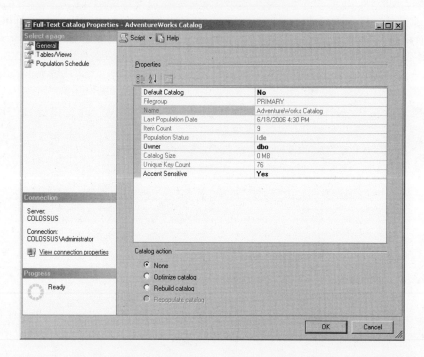

LAB 8
WORKING WITH VIEWS

This lab contains the following exercises and activities:

Exercise 8.1   Designing and Creating a View

Exercise 8.1	Designing and Creating a View
Scenario	You have a database that has been in use for some time and has a number of records in the Contacts table. Your users have asked you to break this data down for them by area code. You have decided that the easiest way to accomplish this goal is to create a view that displays only a subset of data from the table based on the area code.
Duration	This task should take approximately 15 minutes.
Setup	For this exercise, you need access to the machine you installed SQL Server 2005 on in Exercise 2.1 and the AdventureWorks database that is installed with the sample data.
Caveat	Realistically, views won't be this simplistic in the real world; this is just to keep the exercise simple.
Procedure	In this task, you will create a view based on the Person.Contact table in the AdventureWorks database. Specifically, you will create a view that displays only those customers in the 398 area code.
Equipment Used	For this task, you need access to the machine you installed SQL Server 2005 on in Exercise 2.1 and the AdventureWorks database that is installed with the sample data.
Objective	To create the Contacts_in_398 view.
Criteria for Completion	This task is complete when you can query the Contacts_in_398 view and retrieve the correct results.

■ PART A: Designing and Creating a View

1. Open SQL Server Management Studio by selecting it from the Microsoft SQL Server 2005 group under Programs on your Start menu, and connect with Windows Authentication if requested.

2. In Object Explorer, expand your server, and then expand Databases, AdventureWorks. Right-click Views, and select New View.

3. In the Add Table dialog box, select Contact (Person), and click Add.

4. Click Close, this opens the view designer.

5. In the Transact-SQL syntax editor text box, under the column grid, enter the following:

```
SELECT LastName, FirstName, Phone FROM Person.Contact WHERE (Phone LIKE
'398%')
```

6. Click the Execute button (the red exclamation point) on the toolbar to test the query.

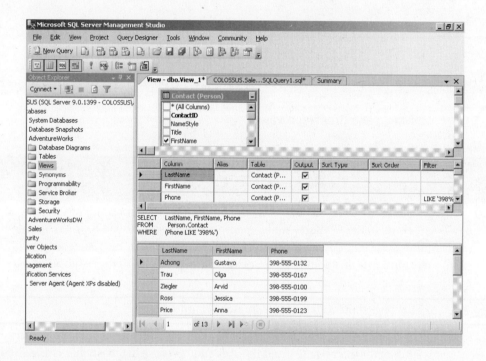

7. Choose File, Save View – dbo.View_1.

8. In the Choose Name dialog box, enter Contacts_in_398, and click OK.

9. To verify that the results are accurate, open a new query, and execute the code used to create the view:

```
USE AdventureWorks SELECT lastname, firstname, phone from Person.Contact
WHERE phone LIKE '398%'
```

Question 1	How can you create a view of the Sales..Customers table to show the Lname, Fname, and Phone using Transact-SQL code?

■ PART B: Verifying Results

1. To test your view, execute this code:

   ```
   USE AdventureWorks SELECT * FROM dbo.Contacts_in_398
   ```

2. You should see only those contacts in the 398 area code.

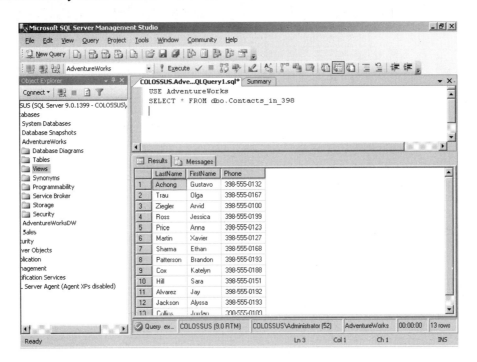

LAB 9
WORKING WITH CONSTRAINTS

This lab contains the following exercises and activities:

Exercise 9.1   Designing and Creating a Constraint

Exercise 9.1	Designing and Creating a Constraint
Scenario	You have just created tables in your new Sales database, one of which holds customer information. You want to make certain that users enter only valid zip codes in the Zip field of the Customers table, so you decide to create a constraint to restrict the data that can be entered in the field.
Duration	This task should take approximately 15 minutes.
Setup	For this exercise, you need access to the machine you installed SQL Server 2005 on in Exercise 2.1, the Sales database you created in Exercise 5.1, and the Customers table you created in Exercise 6.1.
Caveats	This task doesn't have any caveats.
Procedure	In this task, you will create a constraint on the Customers table to prevent users from entering invalid zip codes. Specifically, you will prevent users from entering letters; they can enter only numbers.
Equipment Used	For this exercise, you need access to the machine you installed SQL Server 2005 on in Exercise 2.1, the Sales database you created in Exercise 5.1, and the Customers table you created in Exercise 6.1.
Objective	To create a constraint on the Zip field of the Customers table.
Criteria for Completion	This task is complete when you have a constraint that prevents users from entering letters in the Zip field of the Customers table.

■ PART A: Designing and Creating a Constraint

1. In Object Explorer, expand the Sales database, expand Tables, and then dbo.Customers.
2. Right-click Constraints, and click New Constraint.
3. In the Check Constraints dialog box, enter CK_Zip in the (Name) text box.
4. In the Description text box, enter Check for valid zip codes.
5. To create a constraint that will accept only five numbers that can be zero through nine, enter the following code in the Expression text box:

```
(zip like '[0-9][0-9][0-9][0-9][0-9]')
```

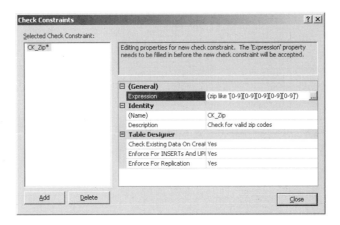

6. Click Close.
7. Click the Save button at the top left of the toolbar.
8. Close the table designer (which opened when you started to create the constraint).

Question 1	How can you force your users to always and only enter "NJ" for the state attribute?

■ PART B: Verifying Results

1. In SQL Server Management Studio, click the New Query button.
2. Enter the following code in the query window:

```
USE Sales INSERT Customers VALUES ('Greg', 'Scott', '111 Main', 'Provo',
'UT', '88102', '5045551212')
```

3. Click the Execute button just above the query window to execute the query, and notice the successful results.
4. To see the new record, click the New Query button, and execute the following code:

```
SELECT * FROM customers
```

5. Notice that the record now exists with a CustID of 1 (because of the identity property discussed earlier in Lab 6, which automatically added the number for you).

6. To test the check constraint by adding characters in the Zip field, click the New Query button, and execute the following code (note the letters in the Zip field):

```
USE Sales INSERT customers VALUES ('Amanda', 'Smith', '817 3rd'
,'Chicago', 'IL', 'AAB1C', '8015551212')
```

7. Notice in the results pane that the query violated a constraint and so failed.

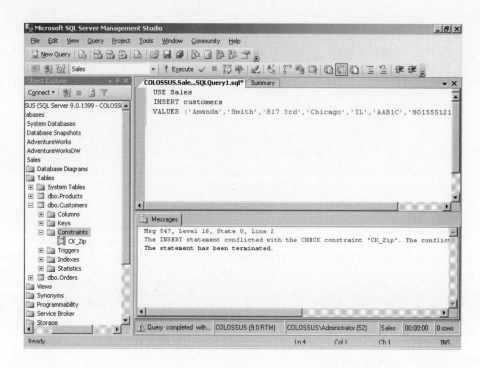

LAB 10
WORKIING WITH
STORED PROCEDURES

This lab contains the following exercises and activities:

Exercise 10.1   Designing and Creating a Stored Procedure

Exercise 10.1	Designing and Creating a Stored Procedure
Scenario	You have a database that has been in use for some time and has a number of records in the Product table. Your users frequently query the table for data based on the SellStartDate column. To speed up execution time and enhance ease of management, you have decided to create a stored procedure that accepts a date as an input parameter and returns a result set of the most frequently queried columns.
Duration	This task should take approximately 15 minutes.
Setup	For this task, you need access to the machine you installed SQL Server 2005 on in Exercise 2.1 and the AdventureWorks database that is installed with the sample data.
Caveat	This task doesn't have any caveats.
Procedure	In this task, you will create a stored procedure based on the Production.Product table in the AdventureWorks database. Specifically, you will create a stored procedure that returns product data based on an input parameter.
Equipment Used	For this task, you need access to the machine you installed SQL Server 2005 on in Exercise 2.1 and the AdventureWorks database that is installed with the sample data.
Objective	To create the Production.Show_Products stored procedure.
Criteria for Completion	This task is complete when you can execute the Production.Show_Products stored procedure using an input parameter and have it return the correct results.

■ PART A: Designing and Creating a Stored Procedure

1. Open SQL Server Management Studio. In Object Explorer, expand your server, and then expand Databases, AdventureWorks, and Programmability.

2. Right-click the Stored Procedures folder icon, and select New Stored Procedure to open a new query window populated with a stored procedure template.

3. In the Transact-SQL syntax box, change the code to look like this:

```
CREATE PROCEDURE Production.Show_Products @Date datetime AS BEGIN SELECT
Name, Color, ListPrice, SellStartDate FROM Production.Product WHERE
SellStartDate > @Date ORDER BY SellStartDate, Name END GO
```

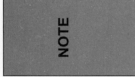 NOTE	*Be sure to name your stored procedures with other than the sp_ prefix. The practice of naming your stored procedures will slow processing in your database.*

4. Click the Execute button on the toolbar to create the procedure.

5. Close the query window.

■ PART B: Verifying Results

1. Execute the following code in a new query window to test your stored procedure:

```
USE AdventureWorks EXEC Production.Show_Products '1/1/1998'
```

2. You should see only those products that are available after January 1, 1998.

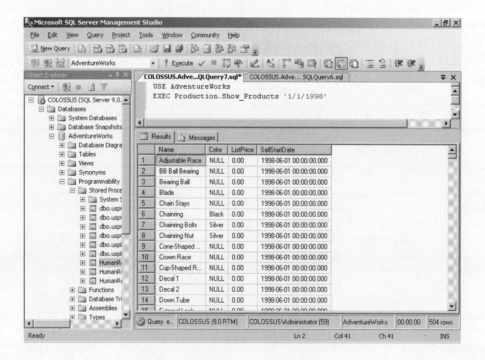

LAB 11
WORKING WITH TRIGGERS

This lab contains the following exercises and activities:

Exercise 11.1	Designing and Creating an Insert Trigger
Exercise 11.2	Designing and Creating a Delete Trigger
Exercise 11.3	Designing and Creating an Update Trigger
Exercise 11.4	Designing and Creating an Instead Of Trigger

Exercise 11.1	Designing and Creating an Insert Trigger
Scenario	You have created a database for your sales department that contains information about orders customers have placed. The sales manager needs to know what is in stock at all times, so she would like to have the quantity of an item that is in stock decremented automatically when a user places an order. You have decided that the best way to accomplish this is by using a trigger on the Orders table.
Duration	This task should take approximately 30 minutes.
Setup	For this task, you need access to the machine you installed SQL Server 2005 on in Exercise 2.1, the Sales database you created in Exercise 5.1, and the Products table you created in Exercise 6.1.
Caveats	When executing a trigger, SQL Server uses two special tables: inserted and deleted. The inserted table holds new records that are about to be added to the table, and the deleted table holds records that are about to be removed. You will be using the inserted table in this task.

Procedure	In this task, you will create a trigger that automatically decrements the InStock quantity in the Products table when a user places an order.
Equipment Used	For this task, you need access to the machine you installed SQL Server 2005 on in Exercise 2.1, the Sales database you created in Exercise 5.2, and the Products table you created in Exercise 6.1.
Objective	To add some data to the Customers and Products tables.
Criteria for Completion	This task is complete when you have a trigger that automatically updates the InStock column of the Products table whenever a record is inserted in the Orders table.

■ PART A: Designing and Creating an Insert Trigger

1. Open SQL Server Management Studio by selecting it from the Microsoft SQL Server 2005 group in Programs on the Start menu, and log in using either Windows Authentication or SQL Server Authentication.

2. Open a new SQL Server query window, and enter and execute the following code to populate the Customers table with customer information:

```
USE Sales

INSERT customers VALUES ('Andrea','Elliott', '111 Main', 'Oakland', 'CA',
'94312', '7605551212')

INSERT customers VALUES ('Tom', 'Smith', '609 Georgia', 'Fresno', 'CA',
'33045', '5105551212')

INSERT customers VALUES ('Janice', 'Thomas', '806 Star', 'Phoenix', 'AZ',
'85202', '6021112222')
```

3. To populate the Products table with product and inventory information, enter and execute the following code:

```
INSERT Products VALUES ('Giant Wheel of Brie', 200)

INSERT Products VALUES ('Wool Blankets', 545)

INSERT Products VALUES ('Espresso Beans', 1527)

INSERT Products VALUES ('Notepads', 2098)
```

4. Close the query window.

■ PART B: Creating the new InvUpdate trigger

1. In Object Explorer, expand your server, and then expand Databases, Sales, Tables, and then dbo.Orders.

2. Right-click the Triggers folder, and select New Trigger.

> NOTE
>
> *As you noticed in the last exercise and as you see now, you must understand Transact-SQL statements even when using the graphical user interface.*

3. In the Transact-SQL syntax box, enter and execute the following code to create the trigger: `CREATE TRIGGER dbo.InvUpdate ON dbo.Orders FOR INSERT AS BEGIN UPDATE p SET p.instock = (p.instock - i.qty) FROM Products p JOIN inserted i ON p.prodid = i.prodid END GO`

4. Close the query window.

■ PART C: Verifying Results

1. Open a new SQL Server query and execute the following code to verify the InStock quantity for item 1 (it should be 200):

   ```
   USE Sales SELECT prodid, instock FROM Products
   ```

2. To cause the INSERT trigger to fire, you need to insert a new record in the Orders table. To do this, open a new query window, and enter and execute the following code, which assumes you're selling 15 quantities of product 1 to customer ID 1 on today's date (GETDATE() is used to return today's date):

   ```
   USE Sales INSERT Orders VALUES (1,1,15,getdate())
   ```

3. To verify that the INSERT trigger fired and removed 15 from the InStock column of the Products table, click the New Query button, and enter and execute the following code:

   ```
   USE Sales SELECT prodid, instock FROM Products
   ```

4. Notice that the exact quantity you sold to customer 1 (15) was subtracted from the total InStock quantity of product ID 1. You now have 185 instead of 200.

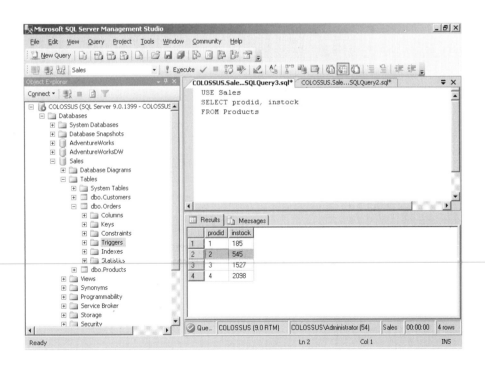

5. Close the query windows.

Exercise 11.2	Designing and Creating a Delete Trigger
Scenario	You have created a database for your sales department that contains information about orders customers have placed. One of your biggest customers is in Arizona, and they have recently had to stop placing regular orders with you, which makes them look inactive. Your sales manager is concerned that someone new may accidentally delete important information about this customer, and she has asked you to prevent that from happening. You have decided that the best way to accomplish this is by using a trigger on the Customers table.
Duration	This task should take approximately 15 minutes.
Setup	For this task, you need access to the machine you installed SQL Server 2005 on in Exercise 2.1, the Sales database you created in Exercise 5.1, and the Customers table you created in Exercise 6.1.
Caveat	When executing a trigger, SQL Server uses two special tables named inserted and deleted. The inserted table holds new records that are about to be added to the table, and the deleted table holds records that are about to be removed. You will be using the deleted table in this task.
Procedure	In this task, you will create a DELETE trigger that prevents users from deleting customers based in Arizona.
Equipment Used	For this task, you need access to the machine you installed SQL Server 2005 on in Exercise 2.1, the Sales database you created in Exercise 5.1, and the Products table you created in Exercise 6.1.
Objective	To create the new AZDel trigger.
Criteria for Completion	This task is complete when you have a trigger that prevents you from deleting customers who reside in Arizona.

■ PART A: Designing and Creating a Delete Trigger

1. In Object Explorer, expand your server, and then expand Databases, Sales, Tables, and dbo.Orders.
2. Right-click the Triggers folder, and select New Trigger.
3. In the Transact-SQL syntax box, enter and execute the following code to create the trigger:

```
CREATE TRIGGER dbo.AZDel ON dbo.Customers FOR DELETE AS BEGIN IF (SELECT
state FROM deleted) = 'AZ' BEGIN PRINT 'Cannot remove customers from AZ'
PRINT 'Transaction has been cancelled' ROLLBACK END END GO
```

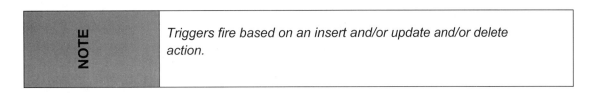

NOTE	*Triggers fire based on an insert and/or update and/or delete action.*

4. Close the query window.

■ PART B: Verifying Results

1. Open a new SQL Server query, and execute the following code to verify you have customers from Arizona (for example, Janice Thomas should be in Arizona):

```
USE Sales SELECT * FROM customers
```

2. To cause the DELETE trigger to fire, try to delete Janice from the Customers table. To do this, open a new query, and enter and execute the following code (you should see an error message upon execution):

```
USE Sales DELETE from Customers WHERE Lname = 'Thomas'
```

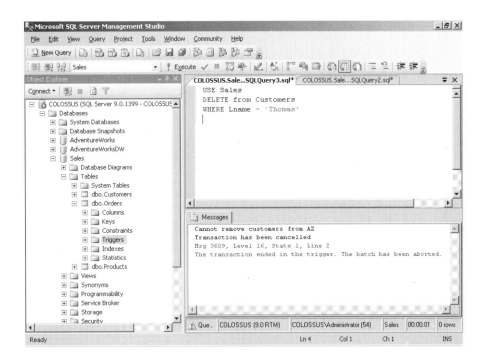

3. To verify that Janice has not been deleted, enter and execute the following code (you should still see Janice):

```
USE Sales SELECT * FROM Customers
```

4. Close the query window.

Exercise 11.3	Designing and Creating an Update Trigger
Scenario	You have created a database for your sales department that contains product information. Some of the new sales personnel have accidentally oversold some product, and the sales manager has asked you for a technical means to prevent this in the future. You have decided to put a trigger in place that prevents users from selling any amount of product that will set the InStock column to a negative value. If they try to execute such a transaction, you have opted to use the RAISERROR() command to write an event to the Windows event log for tracking and reporting purposes.
Duration	This task should take approximately 30 minutes.
Setup	For this task, you need access to the machine you installed SQL Server 2005 on in Exercise 2.1, the Sales database you created in Exercise 5.1, and the Products table you created in Exercise 6.1.
Caveat	When executing a trigger, SQL Server uses two special tables named inserted and deleted. The inserted table holds new records that are about to be added to the table, and the deleted table holds records that are about to be removed. You will be using the inserted table in this task.
Procedure	In this task, you will create a trigger that prevents users from updating a record in the Products table if that update would set the InStock column to a negative amount. If they try to execute such a query, you will use the RAISERROR() command to write an event to the Windows event log.
Equipment Used	For this task, you need access to the machine you installed SQL Server 2005 on in Exercise 2.1, the Sales database you created in Exercise 5.1, and the Products table you created in Exercise 6.1.
Objective	To create the new CheckStock trigger.
Criteria for Completion	This task is complete when you have a trigger that prevents you from entering a negative value in the InStock column of the Products table in the Sales database and also writes an event to the Windows event log if you try.

■ PART A: Designing and Creating an Update Trigger

1. Expand your server, and then expand Databases, Sales, Tables, and then dbo.Products.

2. Right-click the Triggers folder, and select New Trigger.

3. In the Transact-SQL syntax box, enter and execute the following code to create the trigger:

```
CREATE TRIGGER dbo.CheckStock ON dbo.Products FOR UPDATE AS

BEGIN IF (SELECT InStock from inserted) < 0

BEGIN  PRINT  'Cannot  oversell  Products'  PRINT  'Transaction  has  been
cancelled' ROLLBACK RAISERROR('Cannot oversell products', 10, 1) WITH LOG
END

END

GO
```

4. Close the query window.

■ PART B: Verifying Results

1. Open a new SQL Server query, and execute the following code to verify the quantity in stock on available products (product ID 2 should have 545 in stock currently):

```
USE Sales SELECT prodid, instock FROM Products
```

2. To cause the UPDATE trigger to fire, you'll try to sell 600 units of product ID 2 (wool blankets) to a customer. Open a new SQL Server query, and enter and execute the following code (you should see an error message upon execution):

```
USE Sales UPDATE Products SET InStock = (Instock - 600) WHERE prodid = 2
```

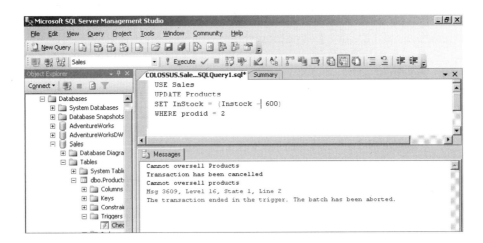

3. To verify that the transaction was disallowed and that you still have 545 wool blankets in stock, click the New Query button, and enter and execute the following code (you should still see 545 of product ID 2):

```
USE Sales SELECT prodid, instock FROM Products
```

4. Now, open Event Viewer, and look in the Application log for the event written by RAISERROR().

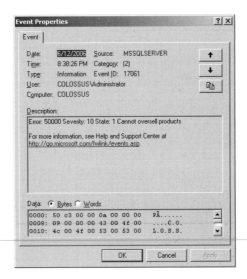

5. Close the query window.

Question 1	Why use triggers? Why were they invented in the first place?

Exercise 11.4	Designing and Creating an Instead of Trigger
Scenario	You have created a database for your sales department with a table that contains customer information. Your sales manager has asked you to make it easier for sales representatives to find the customer data they need, so you have decided to create a view that displays only the necessary data. You need to make sure the sales representatives can insert new data through the view, and because the view does not show all the required columns, you need to create an INSTEAD OF trigger to modify the INSERT statement so that INSERT statements on the view will succeed.
Duration	This task should take approximately 30 minutes.
Setup	For this task, you need access to the machine you installed SQL Server 2005 on in Exercise 2.1, the Sales database you created in Exercise 5.1, and the Customers table you created in Exercise 6.1.
Caveats	This task doesn't have any caveats.
Procedure	In this task, you will create a view that shows only a subset of columns from the Customers table in the Sales database. Then you will create a trigger that intercepts an INSERT statement and modifies the statement so that all required columns are filled in.
Equipment Used	For this task, you need access to the machine you installed SQL Server 2005 on in Exercise 2.1, the Sales database you created in Exercise 5.1, and the Customers table you created in Exercise 6.1.
Objective	To create a view based on the Customers table that does not display the City field (which is a required field for an INSERT).
Criteria for Completion	This task is complete when you have an INSTEAD OF trigger that intercepts an INSERT statement on the PHX_Customers database and adds a value to insert into the City field.

■ PART A: Creating a View

1. In SQL Server Management Studio, open a new query, and enter and execute the following code:

```
USE Sales
GO
CREATE VIEW PHX_Customers AS SELECT fname, lname, address, state, zip,
phone FROM Customers WHERE City = 'Phoenix'
```

2. To verify that the view displays only the columns you want, click the New Query button, and enter and execute the following query:

```
USE Sales SELECT * FROM PHX_Customers
```

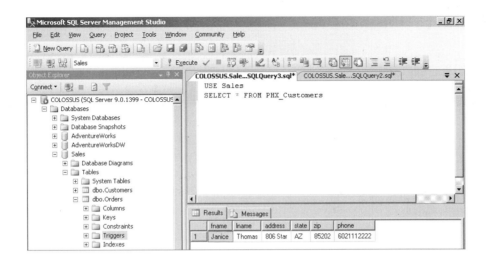

3. Now you will try to insert a new customer through the view. Select New Query with Current Connection from the Query menu, and enter and execute the following code:

```
USE Sales
GO
INSERT PHX_Customers VALUES ('Timothy', 'Calunod', '123 Third', 'AZ',
'85002', '6022221212')
```

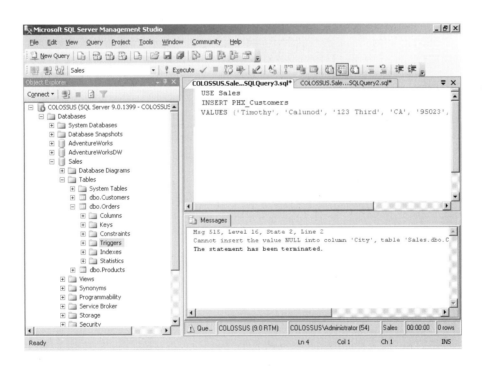

■ PART B: Creating an Instead of Trigger that Inserts the Missing Value for You When You Insert Through the View

1. Expand your server, and then expand Databases, Sales, Views, and then dbo.PHX_Customers.
2. Right-click the Triggers folder, and select New Trigger.
3. In the Transact-SQL syntax box, enter and execute the following code to create the trigger:

```
CREATE TRIGGER Add_City ON PHX_Customers INSTEAD OF INSERT AS DECLARE
@FNAME VARCHAR(20), @LNAME VARCHAR(20), @ADDR VARCHAR(50), @CITY
VARCHAR(20), @STATE NCHAR(2), @ZIP CHAR(5), @PHONE CHAR(10)

SET @CITY = 'Phoenix'

SET @FNAME = (SELECT FNAME FROM INSERTED)

SET @LNAME = (SELECT LNAME FROM INSERTED)

SET @ADDR = (SELECT ADDRESS FROM INSERTED)

SET @STATE = (SELECT STATE FROM INSERTED)

SET @ZIP = (SELECT ZIP FROM INSERTED)

SET @PHONE = (SELECT PHONE FROM INSERTED)

INSERT CUSTOMERS VALUES(@FNAME, @LNAME, @ADDR, @CITY, @STATE, @ZIP,
@PHONE)
```

NOTE	*Caution that DDL triggers are always after triggers. DML triggers, as used here, can be before or after triggers.*

■ PART C: Verifying Results

1. Enter and execute the same code from Step 3 in the previous series of steps:

```
USE Sales INSERT PHX_Customers VALUES ('Timothy', 'Calunod', '123 Third',
'AZ', '85002', '6052221212')
```

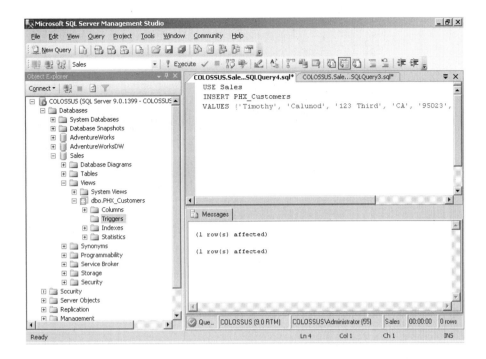

2. To check that the data was inserted into the Customers table and that the City column was populated, select New Query with Current Connection from the Query menu, and enter and execute the following query:

```
USE Sales SELECT * FROM Customers
```

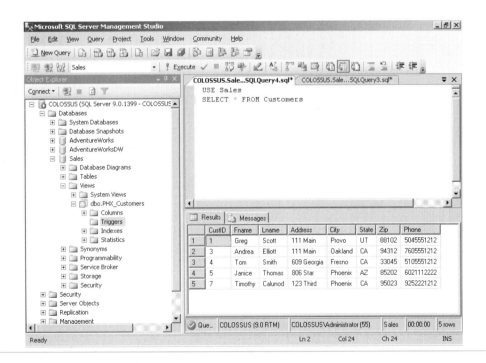

3. Close the query windows.

LAB 12
WORKING WITH FUNCTIONS

This lab contains the following exercises and activities:

Exercise 12.1   Designing and Creating a User-Defined Function

Exercise 12.1	Designing and Creating a User-Defined Function
Scenario	You have created a database for your sales department with a table that contains order information. Your sales manager wants to know the largest number of items for a given product on a single order. She wants to run this calculation every week, so you decide to create a user-defined function for ease of use and management.
Duration	This task should take approximately 15 minutes.
Setup	For this task, you need access to the machine you installed SQL Server 2005 on in Exercise 2.1, the Sales database you created in Exercise 5.1, and the Orders and Customers tables you created in Exercise 6.1.
Caveat	This task doesn't have any caveats.
Procedure	In this task, you will create a user-defined function that calculates the largest number of items for a given product on a single order. First you will add some orders to the database, and then you will create a function to calculate the sales; finally, you will verify the function.
Equipment Used	For this task, you need access to the machine you installed SQL Server 2005 on in Exercise 2.1, the Sales database you created in Exercise 5.1, and the Orders and Customers tables you created in Exercise 6.1.
Objective	To place some orders in the Orders table so the function has some data to work with and then to create the function.
Criteria for Completion	This task is complete when you have created a function that tells you the largest amount of items for a specific product placed on a single order.

■ PART A: Inserting Data in the Orders Table

1. Open a new SQL Server query, and execute the following code to insert some new records in the Orders table:

```
USE Sales
GO
INSERT Orders VALUES (3,2,15,getdate())
GO
INSERT Orders VALUES (1,2,10,getdate())
GO
INSERT Orders VALUES (1,1,20,getdate())
GO
INSERT Orders VALUES (4,3,25,getdate())
GO
```

2. To verify that the new orders exist, enter and execute this code in a new query window:

```
USE Sales SELECT * FROM Orders
```

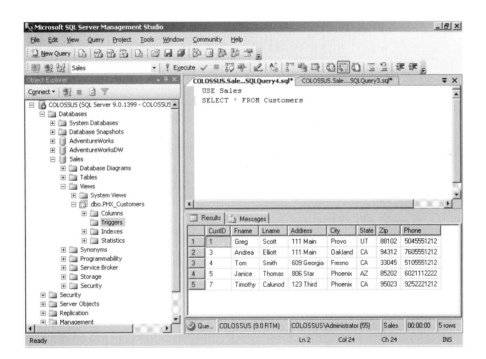

■ PART B: Creating a User-Defined Function to Calculate the Largest Number of Items for a Given Product on a Single Order

1. In SQL Server Management Studio, open a new query, and enter and execute the following code:

```
USE Sales
GO
CREATE   FUNCTION  ItemOrderCount  (@ProductID  int)  RETURNS  int  AS  BEGIN
RETURN (SELECT MAX(Qty) FROM Orders WHERE ProdID = @ProductID) END
```

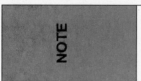 *The CREATE FUNCTION statement must be the first statement in a batch. GO separates the statements into separate batches.*

PART C: Verifying Results

1. Execute the following code:

```
USE Sales
GO
SELECT dbo.ItemOrderCount(1)
```

2. You should get a value of 20; this was the most items placed on a single order for product ID 1.

LAB 13
WORKING WITH TRANSACTIONS AND LOCKS

This lab contains the following exercise and activity:

Exercise 13.1   Identifying and Rectifying the Cause of a Block

Exercise 13.1	Identifying and Rectifying the Cause of a Block
Scenario	You have a SQL Server instance that has been running fine for several months. Recently, though, your developers created some new stored procedures and pushed them into production. When only a few users are connected to the system, everything runs fine, but when the traffic starts to pick up, users start complaining that they cannot access data. The most common complaint is that when the user tries to retrieve data, the system seems to hang and the query never completes. You recognize this as a block, and you decide to troubleshoot it using the sys.dm_exec_requests system view and the KILL command.
Duration	This task should take approximately 20 minutes.
Setup	For this task, you need access to the machine you installed SQL Server 2005 on in Exercise 2.1 and the AdventureWorks database installed with the sample data.
Caveat	This task doesn't have any caveats.

Procedure	In this task, you will simulate a blocking condition using the TABLOCKX and HOLDLOCK query hints. This tells SQL Server to place an exclusive lock on the table and hold the lock until the query completes, which will block other users from accessing the table in question. You will then query the sys.dm_exec_requests system view to find the blocking session ID and use the KILL command to end the session and release the lock.
Equipment Used	For this task, you need access to the machine you installed SQL Server 2005 on in Exercise 2.1 and the AdventureWorks database installed with the sample data.
Objective	To simulate a block, troubleshoot it, and rectify it.
Criteria for Completion	This task is complete when you have simulated a block, queried the sys.dm_exec_requests system view to find the errant session, and used the KILL command to end it.

■ PART A: Setting up the Laboratory Exercise

1. Open SQL Server Management Studio and start a new query.
2. Enter and execute the following Transact-SQL code:

```
USE AdventureWorks
GO
CREATE TABLE dbo.TestTable
(
RowNumber int null,
TextData char(10) null
)
GO
INSERT TestTable (RowNumber) VALUES (1)
GO
```

■ PART B: Identifying and Rectifying the Cause of a Block

1. To start a locking session, open a new query in SQL Server Management Studio, and execute this command:

```
USE AdventureWorks
GO
BEGIN TRAN SELECT * FROM TestTable WITH (TABLOCKX, HOLDLOCK)
```

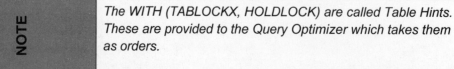

NOTE

The WITH (TABLOCKX, HOLDLOCK) are called Table Hints. These are provided to the Query Optimizer which takes them as orders.

2. Now to create a blocked session, open a new query, and execute this code:

```
USE AdventureWorks
GO
UPDATE TestTable SET TextData = 'test' WHERE RowNumber = 1
```

3. Notice that the second query does not complete because the first query is holding an exclusive lock on the table. To find the session that is doing the blocking, open a third query window.

4. In the third query window, query the sys.dm_exec_requests system view for any session that is being blocked with this code:

```
SELECT session_id, status, blocking_session_id FROM sys.dm_exec_requests
WHERE blocking_session_id > 0
```

5. The blocking_session_id is the session causing the problem. To end it, execute the KILL command with the blocking_session_id value. For example, if blocking_session_id is 53, you would execute this:

```
KILL 53
```

6. Switch to the second query (from Step 2); it should be complete with one row affected.

■ PART C: Verifying Results

1. If you were successful, the query from Step 6 in PART B will complete with one row affected.

LAB 14
MOVING DATA

This lab contains the following exercise and activity:

Exercise 14.1   Using the Copy Database Wizard

Exercise 14.1	Using the Copy Database Wizard
Scenario	Your company has a SQL Server instance in production and another SQL Server instance that is reserved specifically for development and testing. Your developers have been hard at work on a new database for several weeks, and they are now ready to move the database from the development server to the production server. You have decided to use the Copy Database Wizard to accomplish the task.
Duration	This task should take approximately 15 minutes.
Setup	For this task, you need access to the machine you installed SQL Server 2005 on in Exercise 2.1 and the second instance of SQL Server you installed in Exercise 2.2.
Caveat	The SQL Server Agent service must be running on both the default instance and the Second instance for this to be successful.
Procedure	In this task, you'll copy the JobTest database from the default instance of SQL Server to the Second instance using the Copy Database Wizard.
Equipment Used	For this task, you need access to the machine you installed SQL Server 2005 on in Exercise 2.1 and the Second instance of SQL Server you installed in Exercise 2.2.
Objective	To copy the JobTest database using the Copy Database Wizard.
Criteria for Completion	This task is complete when you have successfully copied the JobTest database from the default instance of SQL Server to the Second instance using the Copy Database Wizard.

■ PART A: Creating the JobTest Database

1. Open SQL Server Management Studio by selecting it from the Microsoft SQL Server group. Connect and open a New Query.

2. Enter the following Transact-SQL code into the Query Editor to create the JobTest database:

```
CREATE DATABASE JobTest ON PRIMARY (NAME = JobTest_dat, FILENAME =
'c:\JobTest.mdf', SIZE = 10 MB, MAXSIZE = 15, FILEGROWTH = 10%)
```

3. Click the Execute button.

4. If necessary, click on Databases in Object Explore and press F5 to refresh the display.

■ PART B: Using the Copy Database Wizard

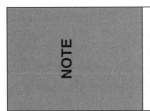

NOTE	*The destination server must be running SQL Server 2005 Service Pack 2 or a later version to use all of the features of the wizard. This exercise uses basic features. Also, the wizard may be run on a computer separate from the source or destination servers.*

1. Open SQL Server Management Studio by selecting it from the Microsoft SQL Server group under Programs on the Start menu, expand your server, and expand Databases.

2. Right-click the JobTest database, go to Tasks, and select Copy Database. You will see the welcome screen.

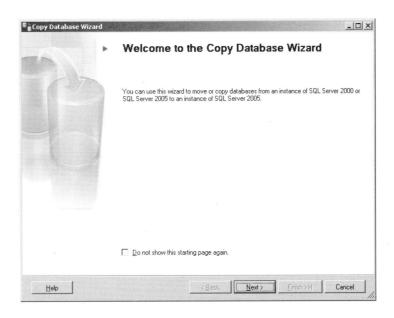

3. Click Next.

4. On the second screen, you are asked to select a source server. Select the default instance of your server and the proper authentication type (usually Windows Authentication), and click Next.

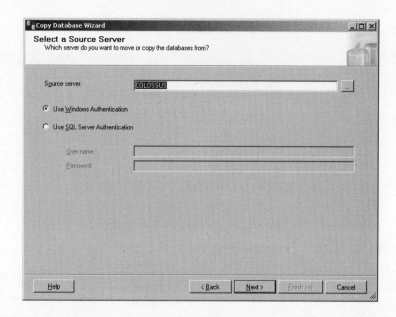

5. On the next screen, you need to select a destination, so click the ellipsis button, check the box next to the Second instance, and click OK. Choose the appropriate security, and click Next.

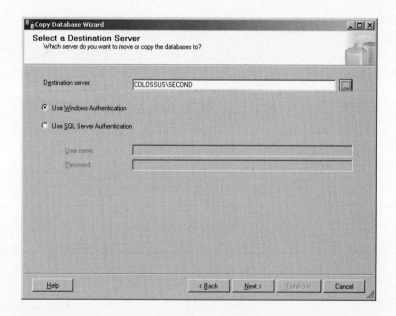

6. Next you are asked which mode you would like to use. Attach/detach is useful for copying databases between servers that are in remote locations from each other; it requires the database to be taken offline. The SQL Management Object transfer method allows you to keep the database online and gives you the flexibility to make a copy on the same server, so select the SQL Management Object Method option, and click Next.

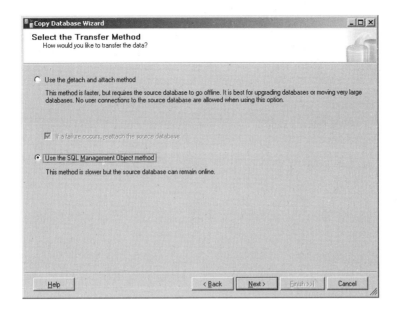

7.   Next you are asked which database you would like to move or copy. Check the Copy box next to JobTest, and click Next.

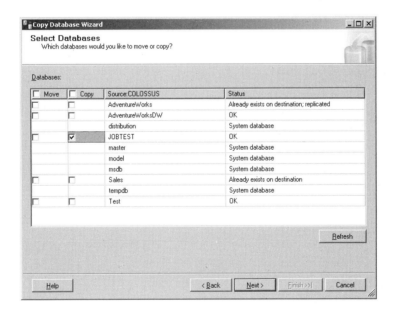

8.   On the Configure Destination Database screen, accept the defaults, and click Next.

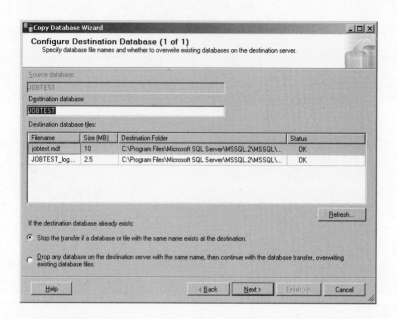

9. On the next screen, you are given the option to copy additional database objects. This is especially useful if the destination server does not have all the logins required to access the database or if additional stored procedures are used for business logic in your applications. Leave the defaults here, and click Next.

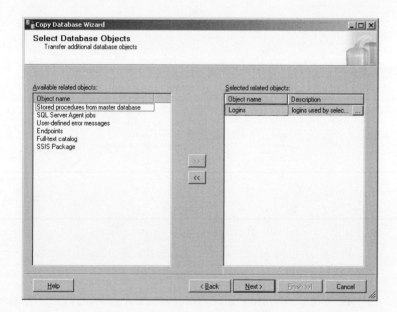

10. You now have the option to change the name of the package that will be created; this matters only if you plan to save the package and execute it later. Accept the defaults, and click Next.

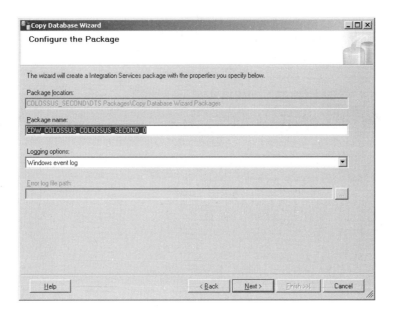

11. On the next screen, you are asked when you would like to run the SSIS job created by the wizard. Select Run Immediately, and click Next.

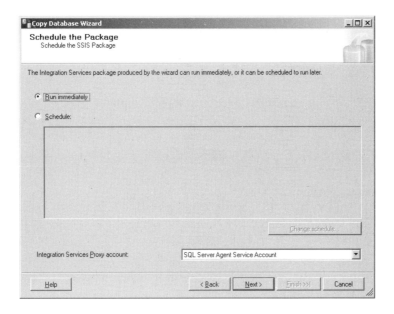

12. The final screen summarizes the choices you have made. Click Finish to copy the Test database.

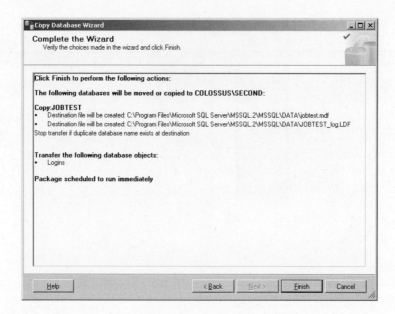

13. You will see the Log Detail screen, which shows you each section of the job as it executes. Clicking the Report button will show each step of the job and its outcome.

14. Click Close on the Performing Operation screen to complete the wizard.

■ PART C: Verifying Results

1. You should see the JobTest database listed in Object Explorer under Databases on the Second instance.

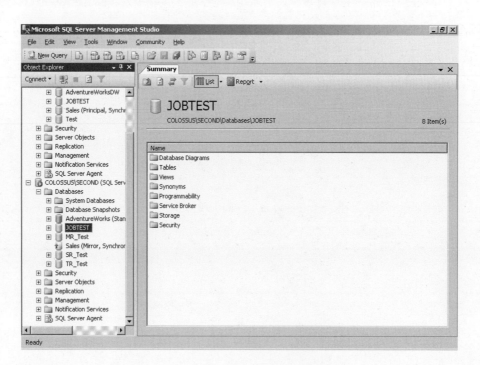

LAB 15
WORKING WITH XML DATA

This lab contains the following exercise and activity:

Exercise 15.1   Using the XML Datatype

Exercise 15.1	Using the XML Datatype
Scenario	Your company has asked you to work with a business-to-business customer who wants to share data using XML. You need to get up to speed using this technology.
Duration	This task should take approximately 30 minutes.
Setup	For this task, you need access to the machine you installed SQL Server 2005 on in Exercise 2.1.and to the database you created in Exercise 5.1.
Caveat	The SQL Server Agent service must be running on both the default instances.
Procedure	In this task, you'll create a new table with a XML datatype column, add some data, and then manipulate the data.
Equipment Used	For this task, you need access to the machine you installed SQL Server 2005 on in Exercise 2.1.
Objective	To create a new table, add, and then manipulate XML data.
Criteria for Completion	This task is complete when you have successfully performed a query method, value method, exist method, and modify method.

■ PART A: Declaring an XML Column

1. In the Connect to Database Engine dialog box, specify the following values and then click Connect.

Property	Value
Server type	Database Engine
Server name	\<YourServerName\>
Authentication	Windows Authentication

2. Use the following code to create a table with an XML column:

```
-- Create a table with an xml column
USE Sales
GO
CREATE TABLE    Invoices
(InvoiceID      int,
SalesDate       datetime,
CustomerID      int,
ItemList        xml);
```

3. On the toolbar, click Execute. This creates a table with a column for untyped XML.

■ PART B: Implicitly Casting a String to XML

1. Use the following code to assign an XML variable and column:

```
-- Use implicit casting to assign an xml variable and column
DECLARE @itemString nvarchar(2000)
SET @itemString = '<Items>
<Item ProductID="2" Quantity="3"/>
<Item ProductID="4" Quantity="1"/>
</Items>'

DECLARE @itemDoc xml
SET @itemDoc = @itemString

INSERT INTO Invoices
VALUES (1, GetDate(), 2, @itemDoc)

INSERT INTO Invoices
VALUES
(1, GetDate(), 2, '<Items>
<Item ProductID="2" Quantity="3"/>
<Item ProductID="4" Quantity="1"/>
</Items>')

SELECT * FROM Invoices
```

2. On the toolbar, click Execute. This code assigns an nvarchar variable to an XML variable and inserts it into the table. The code then inserts a string constant into the XML column directly.

3. Review the results, noting that the XML string has been stored in the table for both INSERT statements.

■ PART C: Inserting a Well-Formed Document

1. Perform the following steps to insert a well-formed document into the XML datatype. This will succeed.

```
-- Well-formed document. This will succeed
INSERT INTO Invoices
VALUES
(1, GetDate(), 2, '<?xml version="1.0" ?>
<Items>
<Item ProductID="2" Quantity="3"/>
<Item ProductID="4" Quantity="1"/>
</Items>')
```

2. On the toolbar, click Execute. This code inserts a well-formed XML document into the table. Then:

```
SELECT * FROM Invoices
```

3. Click Execute. Review the results, noting that the XML string has been stored in the table. Note also that the XML version information is not stored.

■ PART D: Attempting to Insert XML that Is Not Well Formed

1. Perform the following steps to attempt to insert XML that is not well formed into the XML datatype. This will fail.

```
-- Not well-formed. This will fail
INSERT INTO Invoices
VALUES
(1, GetDate(), 2, '<Items>
<Item ProductID="2" Quantity="3"/>
<Item ProductID="4" Quantity="1"/>')
```

2. On the toolbar, click Execute. This code attempts to insert a string that is not well-formed XML into the table.

3. Review the results, noting that the insert failed.

■ PART E: Executing XML Methods

1. Perform the following steps to create a table with an XML column named Invoices and populate the table with data.

```
-- Create a table that includes xml data
USE Sales
CREATE TABLE Stores
(StoreID        integer          IDENTITY PRIMARY KEY,
StoreName       nvarchar(40),
Manager         nvarchar(40),
Invoices        xml)


INSERT INTO Stores
VALUES
('Astro Mountain Bike Company', 'Jeff Adell', '<InvoiceList
xmlns="http://schemas.adventure-works.com/Invoices">
<Invoice InvoiceNo="1000">
<Customer>Kim Abercrombie</Customer>
<Items>
<Item Product="1" Price="1.99" Quantity="2"/>
<Item Product="3" Price="2.49" Quantity="1"/>
</Items>
</Invoice>
<Invoice InvoiceNo="1001">
<Customer>Sean Chai</Customer>
<Items>
<Item Product="1" Price="2.45" Quantity="2"/>
</Items>
</Invoice>
</InvoiceList>')


INSERT INTO Stores
VALUES
('Clocktower Sporting Goods', 'Karen Berge', '<InvoiceList
xmlns="http://schemas.adventure-works.com/Invoices">
<Invoice InvoiceNo="999">
<Customer>Sarah Akhtar</Customer>
<Items>
<Item Product="8" Price="2.99" Quantity="3"/>
</Items>
</Invoice>
```

```
<Invoice InvoiceNo="1000">
<Customer>Bei-Jing Guo</Customer>
<Items>
<Item Product="1" Price="1.95" Quantity="7"/>
<Item Product="100" Price="112.99" Quantity="1"/>
</Items>
</Invoice>
</InvoiceList>')


INSERT INTO Stores
VALUES
('HiaBuy Toys', 'Scott Cooper', NULL)
```

5. On the toolbar, click Execute to execute the entire script.

■ PART F: Examining the Results of the Query Method

1. This code uses the query method in a SELECT statement to retrieve XML data from the Invoices column.

```
-- Use the query method
SELECT StoreName, Invoices.query('declare default element namespace
"http://schemas.adventure-works.com/Invoices";
<SoldItems>
{ for $i in /InvoiceList/Invoice/Items/Item
return $i }
</SoldItems>') SoldItems
FROM Stores
```

2. In the results pane, examine the results returned by the SELECT statement. The result set has two columns, StoreName and SoldItems.

■ PART G: Examining the Results of the Value Method

1. This code uses the value method in a SELECT statement to retrieve a single value from the Invoices column.

```
-- Use the value method
SELECT StoreName, Invoices.value('declare default element namespace
"http://schemas.adventure-works.com/Invoices";
(InvoiceList/Invoice/@InvoiceNo)[1]', 'int') FirstInvoice
FROM Stores
```

2. In the results pane, examine the results returned by the SELECT statement. The result set has two columns, StoreName and FirstInvoice.

■ PART H: Examining the Results of the Exist Method

1. This code uses the exist method in a SELECT statement to find rows that contain an Invoice element in the Invoices column.

```
-- Use the exist method
SELECT StoreName StoresWithInvoices
FROM Stores
WHERE Invoices.exist('declare default element namespace
"http://schemas.adventure-works.com/Invoices";
InvoiceList/Invoice') = 1
```

2. In the results pane, examine the results returned by the SELECT statement. The result set has one column named StoresWithInvoices.

■ PART I: Examining the Results of Binding Relational Columns

1. This code uses the query method in a SELECT statement to retrieve XML data that includes the StoreName relational column.

```
-- Bind a relational column
SELECT Invoices.query('declare default element namespace
"http://schemas.adventure-works.com/Invoices";
<Invoices>
<Store>{sql:column("StoreName")}</Store>
{ for $i in /InvoiceList/Invoice
return $i }
</Invoices>') InvoicesWithStoreName
FROM Stores
```

2. In the results pane, examine the results returned by the SELECT statement. (The result set has a single column, InvoicesWithStoreName.)

■ PART J: Examining the Results of Using the Modify Method to Insert XML

1. Use the modify method to insert XML. This code uses the modify method in an UPDATE statement to insert a SalesPerson element into the Invoice column. The modified XML is then returned by a SELECT statement.

```
-- Use the modify method to insert xml
UPDATE Stores
SET Invoices.modify('declare default element namespace
"http://schemas.adventure-works.com/Invoices";
insert element SalesPerson {"Alice"}
as first into (/InvoiceList/Invoice)[1]')
WHERE StoreID = 1
```

> **NOTE**
>
> *You have learned that T-SQL code is case insensitive but that is not necessarily true of CLR code. Try this: change the word insert above to INSERT. Block this code segment and check the syntax (CTRL-F5 or click the blue checkmark next to the execute button in the Query Editor). The code passes. Now Execute. The code fails. You now know that the syntax check itself is case insensitive even when the code itself is case sensitive.*

```
SELECT Invoices.query('declare default element namespace
"http://schemas.adventure-works.com/Invoices";
(InvoiceList/Invoice)[1]') InsertedSalesPerson
FROM Stores WHERE StoreID = 1
```

2. In the results pane, examine the results returned by the SELECT statement. The result set has a single column, InsertedSalesPerson.

■ PART K: Examining the Results of Using the Modify Method to Update XML

1. This code uses the modify method in an UPDATE statement to update a SalesPerson element in the Invoice column. The modified XML is then returned by a SELECT statement.

```
-- Use the modify method to update xml
UPDATE Stores
SET Invoices.modify('declare default element namespace
"http://schemas.adenture-works.com/Invoices";
replace value of (/InvoiceList/Invoice/SalesPerson/text())[1]
with "Holly"') WHERE StoreID = 1

SELECT Invoices.query('declare default element namespace
"http://schemas.adventure-works.com/Invoices";
(InvoiceList/Invoice)[1]') UpdatedSalesPerson
FROM Stores
WHERE StoreID = 1
```

2. In the results pane, examine the results returned by the SELECT statement. The result set has a single column, UpdatedSalesPerson.

■ PART L: Examining the Results of Using the Modify Method to Delete XML

1. This code uses the modify method in an UPDATE statement to delete a SalesPerson element in the Invoice column. The modified XML is then returned by a SELECT statement.

```
-- Use the modify method to delete xml
UPDATE Stores
```

```
SET Invoices.modify('declare default element namespace
"http://schemas.adventure-works.com/Invoices";
delete (/InvoiceList/Invoice/SalesPerson)[1]')
WHERE StoreID = 1


SELECT Invoices.query('declare default element namespace
"http://schemas.adventure-works.com/Invoices";
(InvoiceList/Invoice)[1]') DeletedSalesPerson
FROM Stores WHERE StoreID = 1
```

2. In the results pane, examine the results returned by the SELECT statement. The result set has a single column, DeletedSalesPerson.

■ PART M: Examining the Results of Using the Nodes Method

You must perform the following steps to examine the results of using the nodes method:

1. This code uses the nodes method with the APPLY operator to extract relational data from an XML column.

```
-- Use the nodes method to extract relational data
SELECT nCol.value('../../@InvoiceNo[1]', 'int') InvoiceNo,
nCol.value('@Product[1]', 'int') ProductID,
nCol.value('@Price[1]', 'money') Price,
nCol.value('@Quantity[1]', 'int') Quantity
FROM Stores CROSS APPLY Invoices.nodes('declare default element namespace
"http://schemas.adventure-works.com/Invoices";
/InvoiceList/Invoice/Items/Item') AS nTable(nCol)
ORDER BY InvoiceNo
```

2. In the results pane, examine the results returned by the SELECT statement. The result set has four columns; InvoiceNo, ProductID, Price, and Quantity.

3. Close SQL Server Management Studio and Windows Explorer. Click No if prompted to save files when closing SQL Server Management Studio.

LAB 16
SETTING PERMISSIONS

This lab contains the following exercises and activities:

Exercise 16.1	Creating a Windows Login
Scenario	You have just installed a new SQL Server at your company, and you need to make sure the right people have access. Some of these users will be using Windows accounts, so you have decided to create Windows logins in SQL Server for these users.
Duration	This task should take approximately 90 minutes.
Setup	For this task, you need access to the machine you installed SQL Server 2005 on in Exercise 2.1.
Caveat	You will need administrative access to the machine you will be using for this task, because you will be creating new groups and user accounts on the machine.

Procedure	In this task, you will create several Windows user and group accounts and then create Windows logins for these accounts in SQL Server.
Equipment Used	For this task, you need access to the machine you installed SQL Server 2005 on in Exercise 2.1.
Objective	To create the Windows user and group accounts in Computer Management (or Active Directory Users and Computers if you are in a domain with Domain Admin rights).
Criteria for Completion	This task is complete when you have successfully created the Windows login accounts specified in the task.

■ PART A: Creating Users and Local Groups in Windows

1. Open Computer Management in the Administrative Tools group under Programs on the Start menu, expand Local Users and Groups, click Users, and then select Action, New User.

> **NOTE**
> *If you are operating in a domain, open Active Directory Users and Computers.*

2. Create six new users with the criteria from Table 16-1.

Table 16-1
New Users

Username	Description	Password	Must Change	Never Expires
MorrisL	IT	Pa$$w0rd	Deselect	Select
RosmanD	Administration	Pa$$w0rd	Deselect	Select
JohnsonK	Accounting	Pa$$w0rd	Deselect	Select
JonesB	Accounting	Pa$$w0rd	Deselect	Select
ChenJ	Sales	Pa$$w0rd	Deselect	Select
SamuelsR	Sales	Pa$$w0rd	Deselect	Select

> **NOTE**
> *You're the DBA, right? Take advantage. Let the network administrator do all the user maintenance work. Specify the right number of groups and all you have to do is add the groups to SQL Server. Everything else is someone else's concern.*

3. While in Computer Management, create a Local group called Accounting.
4. Add the new users you just created whose Description value is Accounting.
5. While still in Computer Management, create a Local group named Sales.

6. Add all the users whose Description value is Sales.

7. Open Local Security Policy from the Administrative Tools group under Programs on the Start menu.

8. Expand Local Policies, and click User Rights Assignment.

9. Double-click the Allow Log on Locally right, and click Add User or Group.

10. Select the Everyone group, click OK, and then click OK again (on a production machine this is not a best practice; this is only for this exercise).

11. Close the Local Policies tool, and open SQL Server Management Studio.

■ PART B: Adding These Windows Accounts to SQL Server

1. Open SQL Server Management Studio, expand your server, and then expand Security and then Logins.

2. Right-click Logins, and select New Login.

3. In the Login Name box, enter <YourComputerName>\Accounting (the name of the Local group created earlier).

4. Under Defaults, select AdventureWorks as the default database.

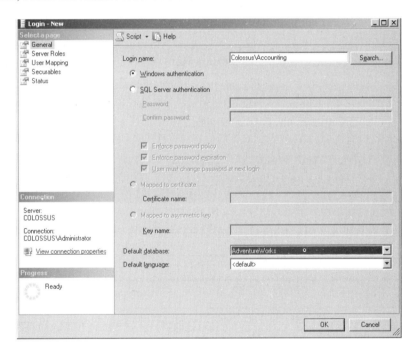

5. On the User Mapping page, select the Map check box next to AdventureWorks to give your user access to the default database.

6. Click OK to create the login.

7. Right-click Logins, and select New Login.

8. In the Login Name box, enter <YourComputerName>\Sales (the name of the Local group created earlier).

9. Under Defaults, select AdventureWorks as the default database.

10. On the User Mapping page, select the Map check box next to AdventureWorks to give your user access to the default database.

11. Click OK to create the login.

12. Right-click Logins, and select New Login.

13. Enter <YourComputerName>\RosmanD in the Login Name field.

14. Under Defaults, select AdventureWorks as the default database.

15. On the User Mapping page, select the Permit check box next to AdventureWorks to give your user access to the default database.

16. Click OK to create the login.

17. Right-click Logins, and select New Login.

18. Enter <YourComputerName>\MorrisL in the Login Name field.

19. Under Defaults, select AdventureWorks as the default database.

20. On the User Mapping page, select the Permit check box next to AdventureWorks to give your user access to the default database.

21. Click OK to create the login.

■ PART C: Verifying Results

1. Log out of Windows, and log back in as JonesB.

2. Open a new SQL Server query in SQL Server Management Studio, and select Windows Authentication from the Authentication drop-down list.

3. Close SQL Server Management Studio, log out of Windows, and log back in as RosmanD.

4. Open a new SQL Server query in SQL Server Management Studio, and select Windows Authentication from the Authentication drop-down list.

Exercise 16.2	Creating a Standard Login
Scenario	You have just installed a new SQL Server at your company, and you need to make sure the right people have access. Some of these users run Macintosh and Linux, and they do not have Windows accounts, so you must create Standard logins in SQL Server for these users.
Duration	This task should take approximately 30 minutes.
Setup	For this task, you need access to the machine you installed SQL Server 2005 on in Exercise 2.1.
Caveats	This task doesn't have any caveats.
Procedure	In this task, you will create two Standard logins in SQL Server.
Equipment Used	For this task, you need access to the machine you installed SQL Server 2005 on in Exercise 2.1.
Objective	To create the Standard logins in SQL Server.
Criteria for Completion	This task is complete when you have successfully created the Standard login accounts specified in the task.

■ PART A: Creating a Standard Login

1. Open SQL Server Management Studio, and expand your server by clicking the + sign next to the icon named after your server.
2. Expand Security, and then expand Logins.
3. Right-click Logins, and select New Login.
4. Select the SQL Server Authentication radio button.
5. In the Name box, enter SmithB.
6. In the Password text box, enter Pa$$w0rd (remember, passwords are case sensitive).
7. In the Confirm Password text box, enter Pa$$w0rd again.
8. Under Defaults, select AdventureWorks as the default database.
9. Uncheck the User Must Change Password at Next Login box.

> **NOTE**
>
> *The two additional check marks are new to SQL Server 2005. They allow you to tic back to the operating system to enforce group policy settings as set for the enterprise network. Try setting Enforce password expiration without checking Enforce password policy.*

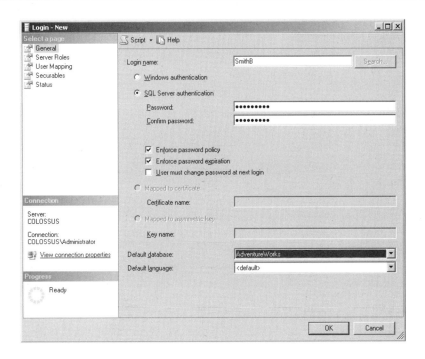

10. On the User Mapping page, select the Map check box next to AdventureWorks to give your user access to the default database.
11. Click OK to create your new login.
12. Right-click Logins, and select New Login.
13. Select the SQL Server authentication radio button.
14. In the Name box, enter GibsonH.
15. In the Password text box, enter Pa$$w0rd.

16. In the Confirm Password text box, enter Pa$$w0rd.

17. Under Defaults, select AdventureWorks as the default database.

18. Uncheck the User Must Change Password at Next Login box.

19. Do not select the Permit check box next to AdventureWorks on the User Mapping page. You'll create a database user account later in this phase.

20. Click OK to create your new login.

■ PART B: Verifying Results

1. To test the SmithB login, click the New Query button in SQL Server Management Studio.

2. On the Query menu, hover over Connection, and then click Change Connection.

3. In the dialog box that opens, select SQL Server Authentication from the Authentication drop-down list.

4. In the Login Name box, enter SmithB.

5. In the Password box, enter Pa$$w0rd.

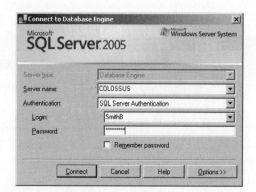

6. Click Connect to connect to AdventureWorks.

Exercise 16.3	Assigning Logins to Fixed Server Roles
Scenario	You have just created several new logins on your SQL Server so your users can access the system. You need to ensure that these accounts have the right amount of administrative access, so you have decided to assign two of these logins to fixed server roles.
Duration	This task should take approximately 15 minutes.
Setup	For this task, you need access to the machine you installed SQL Server 2005 on in Exercise 2.1 and the logins you created in Exercises 16.1 and 16.2.
Caveats	This task doesn't have any caveats.
Procedure	In this task, you will assign two of the logins you created to fixed server roles to limit their administrative access.

Equipment Used	For this task, you need access to the machine you installed SQL Server 2005 on in Exercise 2.1 and the logins you created in Exercises 16.1 and 16.2.
Objective	To assign the logins to fixed server roles.
Criteria for Completion	This task is complete when you have successfully added MorrisL to the sysadmins fixed server role and GibsonH to the serveradmin fixed server role.

■ PART A: Assigning Logins to Fixed Server Roles

1. Open SQL Server Management Studio by selecting it from the SQL Server 2005 group. Under Programs on the Start menu, expand Security, and expand Server Roles.

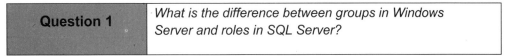

Question 1	*What is the difference between groups in Windows Server and roles in SQL Server?*

2. Double-click the Sysadmin server role to open its properties.

3. Click Add, click Browse, select the check box next to <YourComputerName>\MorrisL, click OK, and then OK again.

4. MorrisL should now appear in the Role Members list.

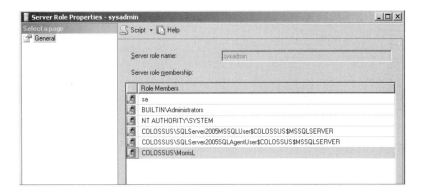

5. Click OK to exit the Server Role Properties dialog box.

6. Double-click Serveradmin Server Role Properties.

7. Click Add, enter GibsonH, and click OK.

8. Click OK to exit the Server Role Properties dialog box.

■ PART B: Verifying Results

1. Connect to Management Studio, expand Security, expand Server roles.

2. Verify that MorrisL is a member of the Sysadmin server role and that GibsonH is a member of the Serveradmin role.

3. MorrisL should show up in the sysadmins Role Members list.

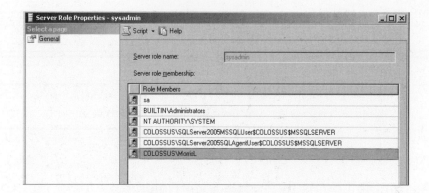

4. GibsonH should show up in the serveradmin Role Members list.

Exercise 16.4	Creating a Database User Mapping
Scenario	You have just created several new logins on your SQL Server so your users can access the system. You didn't create user mappings for all the logins, though, so you need to create a user mapping for GibsonH to access the AdventureWorks database.
Duration	This task should take approximately 15 minutes.
Setup	For this task, you need access to the machine you installed SQL Server 2005 on in Exercise 2.1 and the GibsonH login you created in Exercise 16.2.
Caveats	This task doesn't have any caveats.
Procedure	In this task, you will create a user mapping for GibsonH to access the AdventureWorks database.
Equipment Used	For this task, you need access to the machine you installed SQL Server 2005 on in Exercise 2.1 and the GibsonH login you created in Exercise 16.2.
Objective	To create a user mapping for GibsonH in AdventureWorks.
Criteria for Completion	This task is complete when you have successfully created a user mapping for GibsonH in the AdventureWorks database.

■ PART A: Registering a User with a Database

NOTE	When a user exists in SQL Server the only access to a database is through the Public role. If you remove that user from the Public role, she/he has no access to any database. If users must do more than that allowed by the Public role, you must add them to all databases needed to support their business needs.

1. Open SQL Server Management Studio, and expand your server.
2. Expand Databases by clicking the + sign next to the icon.
3. Expand the AdventureWorks database.
4. Expand Security, and click the Users icon.
5. Right-click Users, and select New User.
6. Click the ellipsis button next to the Login Name box, and click Browse. View all the available names; note that only logins you've already created are available.
7. Select the check box next to GibsonH, and click OK twice.
8. Enter GibsonH in the User Name box and dbo in the Default Schema box.

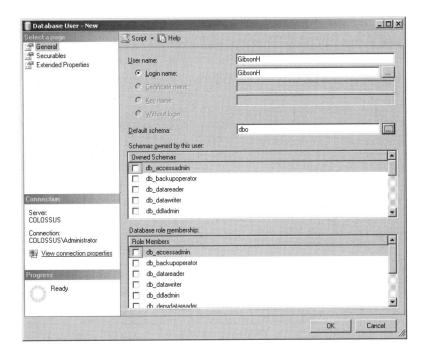

9. Click OK to create the GibsonH database user account.

■ PART B: Verifying Results

1. In Management Studio migrate to the AdventureWorks database, expand Security and then Users.
2. Validate that GibsonH is now listed.

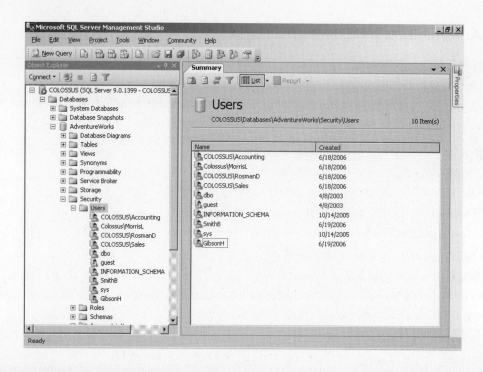

Exercise 16.5	Assigning User Mappings to Fixed Database Roles
Scenario	You have just created several new logins on your SQL Server and created user mappings for them in the AdventureWorks database. You now need to make sure these users have only the necessary permissions, so you need to add some of them to fixed database roles.
Duration	This task should take approximately 15 minutes.
Setup	For this task, you need access to the machine you installed SQL Server 2005 on in Exercise 2.1, the GibsonH and SmithB logins you created in Exercise 16.2, the SmithB user mapping you created in Exercise 16.2, and the GibsonH user mapping you created in Exercise 16.4.
Caveats	This task doesn't have any caveats.
Procedure	In this task, you will add the SmithB user mapping to the db_denydatawriter fixed database role and the GibsonH user mapping to the db_denydatareader fixed database role.
Equipment Used	For this task, you need access to the machine you installed SQL Server 2005 on in Exercise 2.1, the GibsonH and SmithB logins you created in Exercise 16.2, the SmithB user mapping you created in Exercise 16.2, and the GibsonH user mapping you created in Exercise 16.4.
Objective	To add these user mappings to the fixed database roles.
Criteria for Completion	This task is complete when you have successfully added the SmithB user mapping to the db_ denydatawriter fixed database role and the GibsonH user mapping to the db_denydatareader fixed database role.

■ PART A: Assigning a User to a Database Role

1. Open SQL Server Management Studio, expand your server, and then expand Databases and then AdventureWorks.
2. Expand Security, then Roles, and then Database Roles.
3. Right-click db_denydatawriter, and select Properties.
4. Click Add.
5. Enter SmithB in the Enter Object Names to Select box, and click OK.

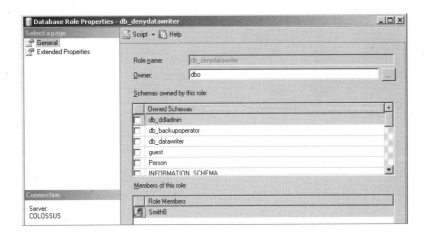

6. Click OK again to return to SQL Server Management Studio.
7. Right-click db_denydatareader, and select Properties.
8. Click Add.
9. Enter GibsonH in the Enter Object Names to Select box, and click OK. Then click OK again.

Question 2	Which is easier, adding a user to a database role or assigning the user permissions?

■ PART B: Verifying Results

1. Open a new SQL Server query in SQL Server Management Studio.
2. On the Query menu, hover over Connection, and then click Change Connection.
3. Select SQL Server Authentication from the Authentication list box.
4. In the User Name box, enter SmithB; in the Password box, enter Pa$$w0rd, and click Connect.
5. Enter and execute the following query, which tries to update information in the Human-Resources.Department table (it fails because SmithB is a member of the db_denydatawriter role):

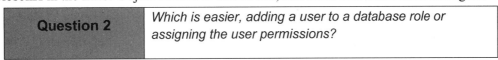

```
INSERT INTO HumanResources.Department (DepartmentID, Name, GroupName,
ModifiedDate) values (200, 'Test','TestGroup',GetDate())
```

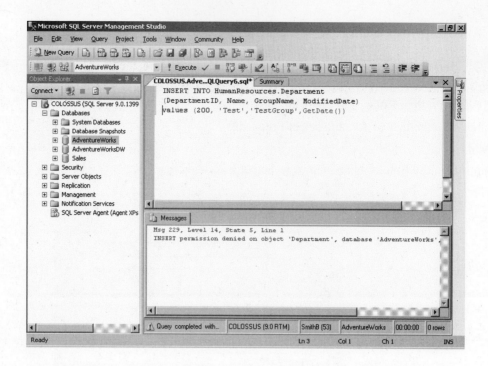

6. On the Query menu, hover over Connection, and then click Change Connection.

7. Select SQL Server Authentication from the Authentication list box.

8. In the User Name box, enter GibsonH; in the Password box, enter Pa$$w0rd, and click Connect.

9. Enter and execute the following query, which tries to read data from the Human-Resources.Department table (it fails because GibsonH is a member of the db_ denydatareader role):

```
SELECT       DepartmentID,       Name,       GroupName,       ModifiedDate       FROM
HumanResources.Department
```

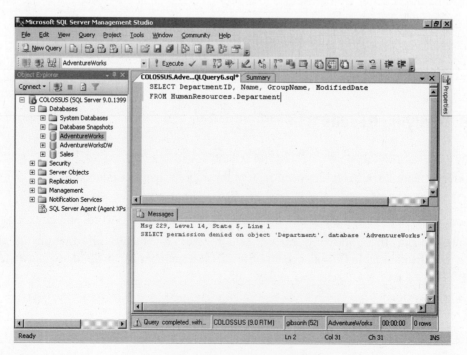

10. Close the query window.

Exercise 16.6	Creating a Custom Database Role
Scenario	You have just created several new logins on your SQL Server and created user mappings for them in the AdventureWorks database. You have added some of these users to fixed database roles, but other users require combinations of permissions that none of the fixed database roles offers. To assign the appropriate permissions to these users, you decide to create a custom database role.
Duration	This task should take approximately 15 minutes.
Setup	For this task, you need access to the machine you installed SQL Server 2005 on in Exercise 2.1, the AdventureWorks database, and the RosmanD login you created in Exercise 16.1.
Caveats	In the real world, you would not create a custom database role for just one user, and you would grant more than a single permission.
Procedure	In this task, you will create a custom database role that grants the members permission to select data from the HumanResources.Department table in the AdventureWorks database. You will then add the RosmanD user mapping to the new custom database role.
Equipment Used	For this task, you need access to the machine you installed SQL Server 2005 on in Exercise 2.1, the AdventureWorks database, and the RosmanD login you created in Exercise 16.1.
Objective	To create a new custom database role and add users to it.
Criteria for Completion	This task is complete when you have successfully created a new custom database role, assigned permissions, and added the RosmanD user mapping to the new role.

■ PART A: Creating a Custom Database Role

1. Open SQL Server Management Studio, expand your server, and then expand Databases and then AdventureWorks.
2. Expand Security and then Roles.
3. Right-click Database Roles, and select New Database Role.
4. In the Role Name box, enter SelectOnly, and enter dbo in the Owner box.
5. Add <YourServerName>\RosmanD to the Role Members list.

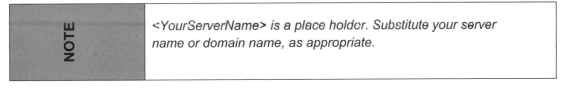

NOTE

<YourServerName> is a place holder. Substitute your server name or domain name, as appropriate.

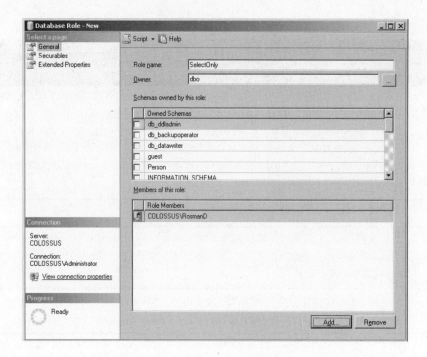

6. On the Securables page, click Add under the Securables list box, select the Specific Objects radio button, and click OK.

7. Click the Objects Type button, select Tables, and click OK.

8. Click Browse, select the HumanResources.Department check box, click OK, and then click OK again.

9. In the Explicit Permissions for HumanResources.Department list, check the Grant check box next to Select.

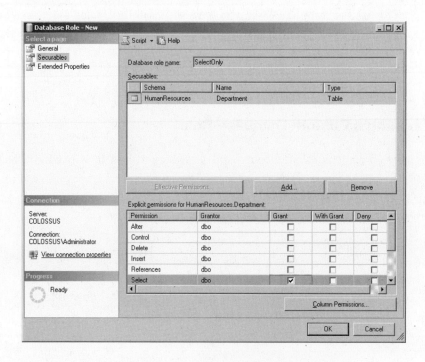

10. Click OK to create the role and return to SQL Server Management Studio.

■ PART B: Verifying Results

1. Close all programs, log out of Windows, and log back in as RosmanD.

2. Open a new SQL Server query in SQL Server Management Studio, and connect using Windows Authentication.

3. Notice that the following query succeeds because RosmanD is a member of the new SelectOnly role:

```
USE AdventureWorks SELECT * FROM HumanResources.Department
```

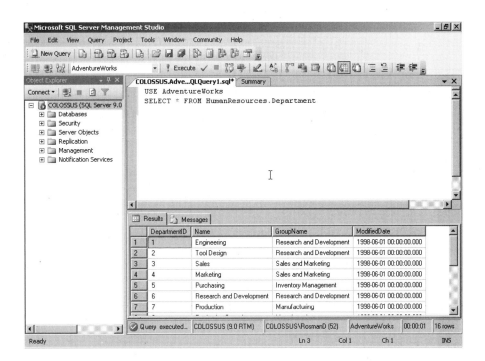

4. Now notice the failure of the next query because RosmanD is a member of a role that is allowed to select only:

```
INSERT INTO HumanResources.Department (DepartmentID, [Name], GroupName,
ModifiedDate) values (200, 'Test','TestGroup',GetDate())
```

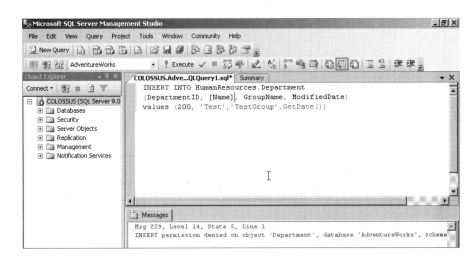

5. Close all programs, log out of Windows, and log back in as yourself.

Exercise 16.7	Creating an Application Role
Scenario	Your company has written a custom application for manipulating data in one of your databases. This application has taken hundreds of staff hours and has cost hundreds of thousands of dollars, so management has insisted employees use this custom application to access the database and nothing else. You have decided the best way to accomplish this goal is to create an application role, which your developers can hard code into their application.
Duration	This task should take approximately 15 minutes.
Setup	For this task, you need access to the machine you installed SQL Server 2005 on in Exercise 2.1 and the AdventureWorks database.
Caveats	This task doesn't have any caveats.
Procedure	In this task, you will create an application role that grants the members permission to select data from the HumanResources.Department table in the AdventureWorks database.
Equipment Used	For this task, you need access to the machine you installed SQL Server 2005 on in Exercise 2.1 and the AdventureWorks database.
Objective	To create an application role and assign permissions to it.
Criteria for Completion	This task is complete when you have successfully created a new application role and assigned permissions.

■ PART A: Creating an Application Role

1. Open SQL Server Management Studio, and expand Databases, AdventureWorks and then Security.
2. Right-click Application Roles, and select New Application Role.
3. In the Role Name box, enter EntAppRole.
4. Enter dbo in the Default Schema box.
5. In the Password and Confirm Password boxes, enter Pa$$w0rd.

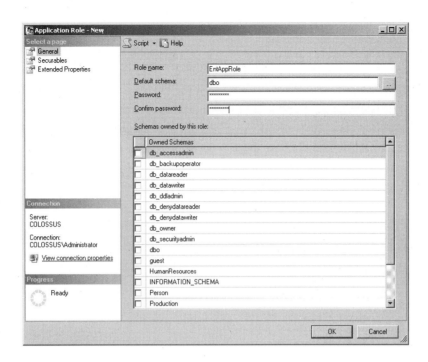

6. On the Securables page, click Add under the Securables list box, select the Specific Objects radio button, and click OK.

7. Click the Objects Type button, select Tables, and click OK.

8. Click Browse, select the HumanResources.Department check box, click OK, and then click OK again.

9. In the Permissions for HumanResources.Department list, select the Grant check box next to Select, and click OK to create the role.

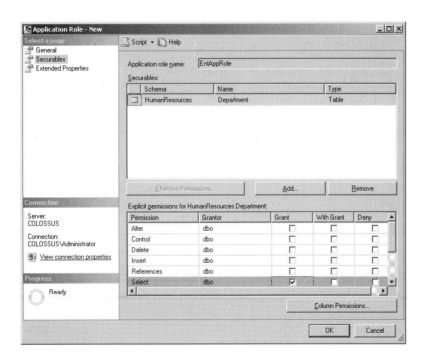

■ PART B: Verifying Results

1. Open a new SQL Server query in SQL Server Management Studio.

2. On the Query menu, hover over Connection, and click Change Connection.

3. Connect using SQL Authentication with GibsonH as the username and Pa$$w0rd as the password.

4. Enter and execute the following query. Notice that it fails because GibsonH has been denied Select permissions because of membership in the db_denydatareader database role (assigned in Exercise 16.5):

```
USE AdventureWorks SELECT * FROM HumanResources.Department
```

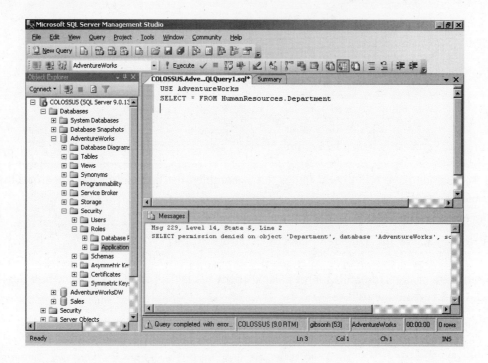

5. To activate the application role, execute the following query:

```
sp_setapprole @rolename='EntAppRole', @password='Pa$$w0rd'
```

6. Clear the query window, and execute the following query. Notice that the query is successful this time. This is because SQL Server now sees you as EntAppRole, which has Select permission.

```
SELECT * FROM HumanResources.Department
```

7. Close the query window.

Exercise 16.8	Assigning Permissions
Scenario	You have just installed a new SQL Server for your company and want to make sure you fully understand how permissions work, so you have decided to test permissions on your test server before assigning them to users on production databases.
Duration	This task should take approximately 30 minutes.
Setup	For this task, you need access to the machine you installed SQL Server 2005 on in Exercise 2.1, the SmithB account you created in Exercise 16.2, and the AdventureWorks database.
Caveats	In a production environment, for ease of management, you will create custom roles and assign permissions to those roles. You will usually assign permissions to a specific user only when you want to deny a permission to that user.
Procedure	In this task, you will assign permissions to the SmithB user mapping. You will then change the permission state and test the effects of the change.
Equipment Used	For this task, you need access to the machine you installed SQL Server 2005 on in Exercise 2.1, the SmithB account you created in Exercise 16.2, and the AdventureWorks database.
Objective	To create assign and modify permissions for SmithB.
Criteria for Completion	This task is complete when you have successfully assigned the permissions as described in the PART A section.

■ PART A: Assigning Permissions

1. Open SQL Server Management Studio, expand your server, and then expand Databases, AdventureWorks, and Security.
2. Expand Users, right-click SmithB, and select Properties.
3. On the Securables page, click Add under the Securables list box, select the Specific Objects radio button, and click OK.
4. Click the Objects Type button, select Tables, and click OK.
5. Click Browse, select the HumanResources.Department check box, and click OK twice.

Question 3	*Do you know what each of these permissions control? Look in Books Online for explanations of any you don't quite know. What specifically does References control? With Grant?*

6. In the Permissions for HumanResources.Department list, select the Grant check box next to Select, and click OK.

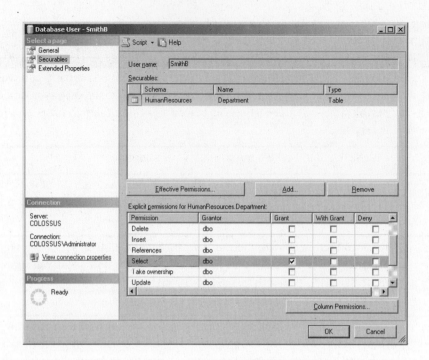

7. Open a new SQL Server query in SQL Server Management Studio.

8. On the Query menu, hover over Connection, and then click Change Connection.

9. Select SQL Server Authentication from the Authentication list box.

10. In the User Name box, enter SmithB; in the Password box, enter Pa$$w0rd, and click Connect.

11. Execute the following query. It's successful because SmithB has Select permission on the HumanResources.Department table.

```
USE AdventureWorks

SELECT * FROM HumanResources.Department
```

12. Right-click SmithB under Users in the AdventureWorks database, and select Properties.

13. On the Securables page, click Add under the Securables list box, select the Specific Objects radio button, and click OK.

14. Click the Objects Type button, select Tables, and click OK.

15. Click Browse, select the HumanResources.Department check box, and click OK twice.

16. In the Permissions for HumanResources.Department list, uncheck the Grant check box next to Select (this revokes the permission), and click OK.

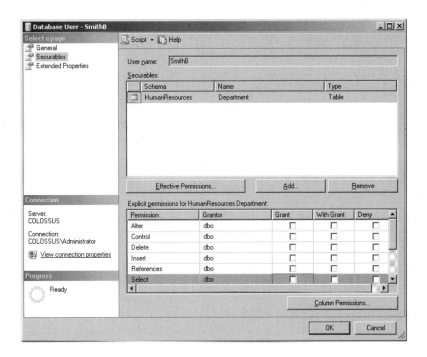

17. Return to the query window, and execute the query in Step 11. It fails because SmithB doesn't have explicit Select permission.

18. Right-click SmithB under Users in the AdventureWorks database, and select Properties.

19. Under Role Membership, select the check box next to the db_datareader role. Click OK.

20. Return to the query window, and rerun the query from Step 11. Now it fails because SmithB does not have the permission expressly applied and is not a member of a role that has this permission.

21. Right-click SmithB under Users in the AdventureWorks database, and select Properties.

22. On the Securables page, click Add under the Securables list box, select the Specific Objects radio button, and click OK.

23. Click the Objects Type button, select Tables, and click OK.

24. Click Browse, select the HumanResources.Department check box, and click OK twice.

25. In the Permissions for HumanResources.Department list, select the Deny check box next to Select, and click OK.

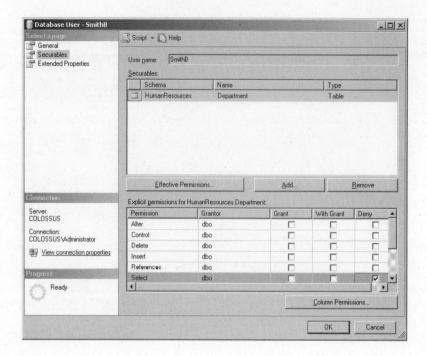

26. Return to the query window, and again run the query from Step 11. It fails this time because you've specifically denied SmithB access.

■ PART B: Verifying Results

1. In Management Studio, expand databases, AdventureWorks, Tables, HumanResources.Department.
2. Right click on HumanResources.Department and select Properties.
3. Click Permissions.
4. Confirm permissions are set as you wish them.

Exercise 16.9	Configuring Encrypted Connections
Scenario	You have just installed a new SQL Server for your company and created a database that holds e-commerce data. For your customers' convenience, your company has decided to store credit card information so users do not have to enter it every time they place an order on your site. You know you need to use the highest level of security possible, so you have decided to configure SQL Server to require encrypted connections.
Duration	This task should take approximately 30 minutes.
Setup	For this task, you need access to the machine you installed SQL Server 2005 on in Exercise 2.1.
Caveats	In production, you should not use a self-signed certificate. You are using one in this task for simplicity's sake.

Procedure	In this task, you will configure SQL Server to use encrypted connections using a self-signed certificate.
Equipment Used	For this task, you need access to the machine you installed SQL Server 2005 on in Exercise 2.1.
Objective	To configure the server to force clients to use encrypted connections.
Criteria for Completion	This task is complete when you can connect to SQL Server using an encrypted connection.

■ PART A: Configuring Encrypted Connections

1. In SQL Server Configuration Manager, expand SQL Server 2005 Network Configuration, right-click Protocols for <server instance>, and then select Properties.
2. In the Protocols for <instance name> Properties dialog box, on the Flags tab, change ForceEncryption to Yes.

3. Click OK twice to close the warning dialog box that opens.
4. Restart the SQL Server service.
5. Again, right-click Protocols for <server instance>, and then select Properties.
6. In the Protocols for <instance name> Properties dialog box, on the Certificate tab, select the desired certificate (in this case the self-signed certificate) from the Certificate dropdown list, and then click OK.

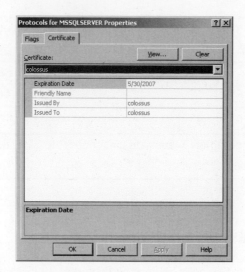

7. Click OK to close the warning dialog box that opens.

8. Restart the SQL Server service. Next, you need to configure the clients to request encrypted connections to the server.

■ PART B: Configuring Clients to Request Encrypted Connections

1. In SQL Server Configuration Manager, right-click SQL Native Client Configuration, and select Properties.

2. On the Flags tab, in the Force Protocol Encryption box, select Yes, and then click OK to close the dialog box.

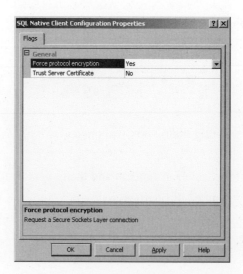

3. Restart the SQL Server service.

■ PART C: Verifying Results

1. Open a new SQL Server query in SQL Server Management Studio.
2. On the Query menu, hover over Connection, and then click Change Connection.
3. Select Windows Authentication from the Authentication list box.
4. Click the Options button, and check the Encrypt Connection box.

5. Click Connect to make the connection.

Question 4	What does it mean to secure a "connection"? Is this the same as configuring IPSEC on the server?

LAB 17
BACKING UP AND RESTORING DATA

This lab contains the following exercises and activities:

Exercise 17.1	Creating a Backup Device
Scenario	You need to start backing up the databases you have created on your new SQL Server. Before you can start backing them up, though, you realize you need a place to store the backups, so you decide to create a backup device for storing backups.
Duration	This task should take approximately 15 minutes.
Setup	For this task, you need access to the machine you installed SQL Server 2005 on in Exercise 2.1.
Caveat	This task doesn't have any caveats.
Procedure	In this task, you will create a backup device.

Equipment Used	For this task, you need access to the machine you installed SQL Server 2005 on in Exercise 2.1.
Objective	To create a backup device.
Criteria for Completion	This task is complete when you have created a new backup device.

■ PART A: Creating a Backup Device

1. Open SQL Server Management Studio by selecting it from the SQL Server 2005 group under Programs on the Start menu. Expand your server, and then expand Server Objects.

2. Right-click Backup Devices in Object Explorer, and select New Backup Device.

3. In the Device Name box of the Backup Device dialog box, enter AdvWorks. Notice that the filename and path are filled in for you; make sure you have enough free space on the drive SQL Server has selected.

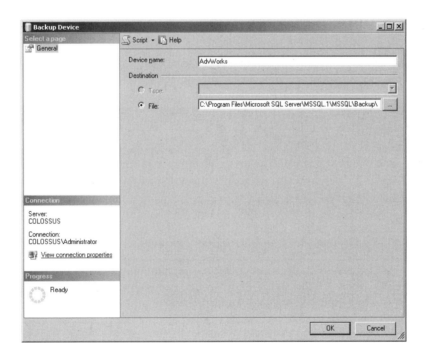

4. Click OK to create the device.

Question 1	What is the advantage of creating a backup device as contrasted with specifying the full path name in a script?

■ PART B: Verifying Results

1. In Object Explorer, under Server Objects and Backup Devices, verify that your new device is listed.

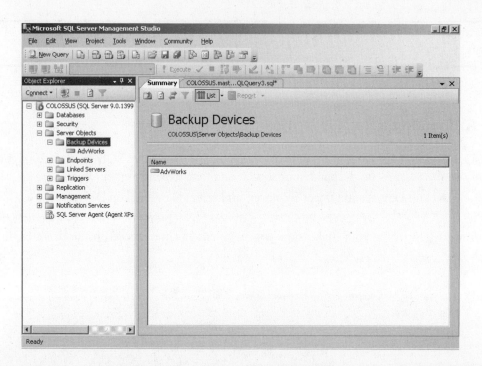

Exercise 17.2	Performing a Full Backup
Scenario	You need to start backing up the databases you have created on your new SQL Server. You know you need a full backup before you can start using differential or transaction log backups, so you decide to create a baseline by performing a full backup.
Duration	This task should take approximately 15 minutes.
Setup	For this task, you need access to the machine you installed SQL Server 2005 on in Exercise 2.1, the AdventureWorks database installed with the sample data, and the AdvWorks backup device you created in Exercise 17.1.
Caveat	This task doesn't have any caveats.
Procedure	In this task, you will perform a full backup on the AdventureWorks database.
Equipment Used	For this task, you need access to the machine you installed SQL Server 2005 on in Exercise 2.1, the AdventureWorks database installed with the sample data, and the AdvWorks backup device you created in Exercise 17.1.
Objective	To perform a full backup of the AdventureWorks database.
Criteria for Completion	This task is complete when you have a full backup of the AdventureWorks database stored in the AdvWorks backup device.

■ PART A: Performing a Full Backup

1. Open SQL Server Management Studio, expand Databases, right-click AdventureWorks, point to Tasks, and click Back Up.

2. In the Backup dialog box, make sure AdventureWorks is the selected database to back up and make sure Backup Type is Full.

3. Leave the default name in the Name box. In the Description box, enter Full Backup of AdventureWorks.

4. Under Destination, a disk device may already be listed. If so, select the device, and click Remove.

5. Under Destination, click Add.

6. In the Select Backup Destination box, click Backup Device, select AdvWorks, and click OK.

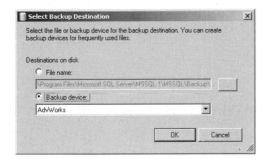

7. You should now have a backup device listed under Destination.

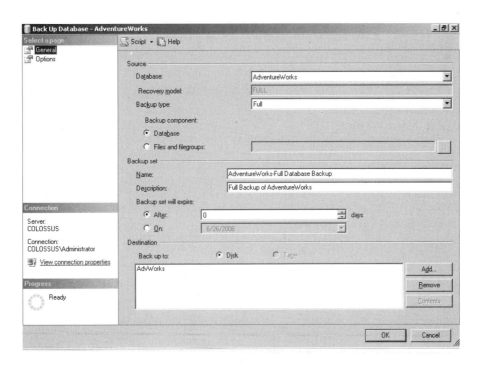

8. Switch to the Options page. On the Options page, select Overwrite All Existing Backup Sets. This option initializes a new device or overwrites an existing one.

9. Select Verify Backup When Finished to check the actual database against the backup copy, and be sure they match after the backup is complete.

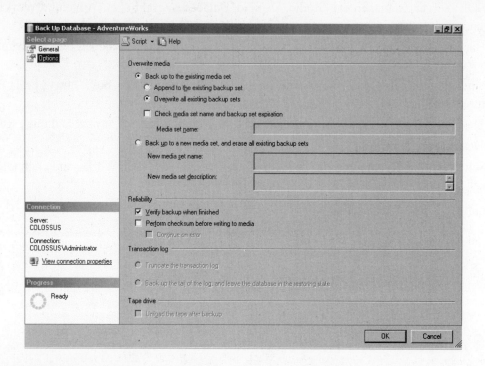

10. Click OK to start the backup.

11. When the backup is complete, you will get a notification; click OK to close it.

Question 2	*A backup is simply a means of creating redundant data; a second copy of your database. Compare with a database snapshot, database mirroring, replication, fail-over clustering, and log shipping. Which is best for differing scenarios?*

■ PART B: Verifying Results

1. To verify the backup, you can look at the contents of the backup device, so expand Backup Devices under Server Objects in Object Explorer.

2. Right-click AdvWorks, and select Properties.

3. On the Media Contents page, you should see the full backup of AdventureWorks.

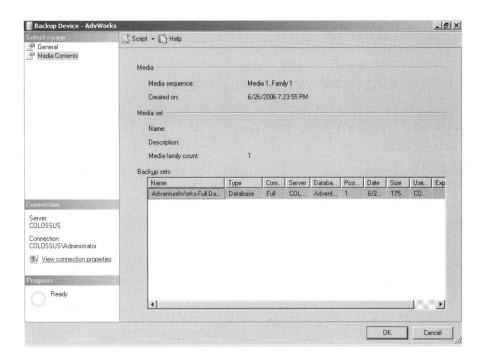

4. Click OK to return to SQL Server Management Studio.

Exercise 17.3	Performing a Differential Backup
Scenario	You have started performing full backups of your databases on a regular basis, and you have noticed that, as the database grows, the backup get slower. You know you need to speed up the backup process, so you decide to incorporate differential backups into your backup scheme.
Duration	This task should take approximately 15 minutes.
Setup	For this task, you need access to the machine you installed SQL Server 2005 on in Exercise 2.1, the AdventureWorks database installed with the sample data, and the AdvWorks backup device you created in Exercise 17.1.
Caveat	This task doesn't have any caveats.
Procedure	In this task, you will perform a differential backup on the AdventureWorks database.
Equipment Used	For this task, you need access to the machine you installed SQL Server 2005 on in Exercise 2.1, the AdventureWorks database installed with the sample data, and the AdvWorks backup device you created in Exercise 17.1.
Objective	To perform a differential backup of the AdventureWorks database.
Criteria for Completion	This task is complete when you have a differential backup of the AdventureWorks database stored in the AdvWorks backup device.

■ PART A: Performing a Differential Backup

1. Open SQL Server Management Studio. Expand your server, and then expand Databases.
2. Right-click AdventureWorks, point to Tasks, and select Back Up.
3. In the Backup dialog box, make sure AdventureWorks is the selected database to back up and Backup Type is Differential.
4. Leave the default name in the Name box. In the Description box, enter Differential Backup of AdventureWorks.
5. Under Destination, make sure the AdvWorks device is listed.

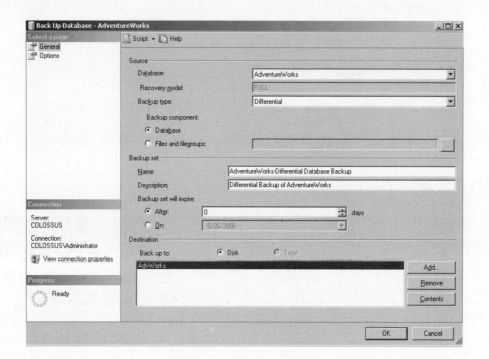

6. On the Options page, make sure Append to the Existing Backup Set is selected so you don't overwrite your existing full backup.
7. On the Options tab, select Verify Backup When Finished.
8. Click OK to start the backup.

Question 3	*Database management is all about trade-offs. If you backup slowly you can restore quickly. A differential backup goes quickly but at the expense having having a full backup and potentially multiple differential backups to process. Which is best?*

■ PART B: Verifying Results

1. To verify the backup, you can look at the contents of the backup device, so expand Backup Devices under Server Objects in Object Explorer.

2. Right-click AdvWorks, and select Properties.
3. On the Media Contents page, you should see the differential backup of AdventureWorks.

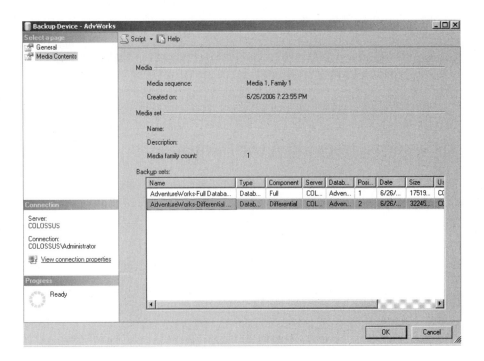

4. Click OK to return to SQL Server Management Studio.

Exercise 17.4	Performing a Transaction Log Backup
Scenario	You have started performing full and differential backups of your databases on a regular basis. You know that if you do not start performing transaction log backups, your users will eventually get locked out of the database when the transaction log fills to capacity. You also want the extra safety measure of having transaction log backups in place, so you decide to start performing transaction log backups.
Duration	This task should take approximately 15 minutes.
Setup	For this task, you need access to the machine you installed SQL Server 2005 on in Exercise 2.1, the AdventureWorks database installed with the sample data, and the AdvWorks backup device you created in Exercise 17.1. Also, the AdventureWorks database must be set to use the Full recovery model as outlined in Exercise 5.2.
Caveat	This task doesn't have any caveats.
Procedure	In this task, you will perform a transaction log backup on the AdventureWorks database.

Equipment Used	For this task, you need access to the machine you installed SQL Server 2005 on in Exercise 2.1, the AdventureWorks database installed with the sample data, and the AdvWorks backup device you created in Exercise 17.1.
Objective	To perform a transaction log backup of the AdventureWorks database.
Criteria for Completion	This task is complete when you have a transaction log backup of the AdventureWorks database stored in the AdvWorks backup device.

■ PART A: Performing a Transaction Log Backup

1. Open SQL Server Management Studio. Expand your server, and then expand Databases.
2. Right-click AdventureWorks, point to Tasks, and select Back Up.
3. In the Backup dialog box, make sure AdventureWorks is the selected database to back up and Backup Type is Transaction Log.
4. Leave the default name in the Name box. In the Description box, enter Transaction Log Backup of AdventureWorks.
5. Under Destination, make sure the AdvWorks device is listed.

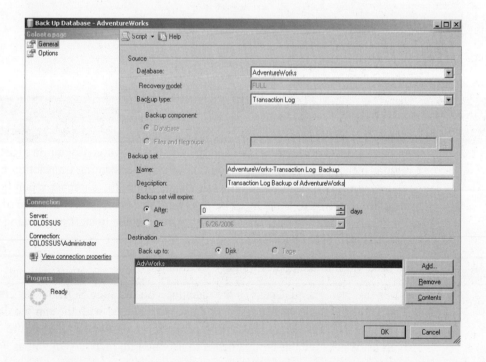

6. On the Options page, make sure Append to the Existing Backup Set is selected so you don't overwrite your existing full backup.
7. On the Options page, select Verify Backup When Finished.
8. Click OK to start the backup.
9. When the backup is complete, you will get a notification; click OK to close it.

Question 4	How often should you perform a log backup?

■ PART B: Verifying Results

1. To verify the backup, you can look at the contents of the backup device, so expand Backup Devices under Server Objects in Object Explorer.
2. Right-click AdvWorks, and select Properties.
3. On the Media Contents page, you should see the transaction log backup of AdventureWorks.

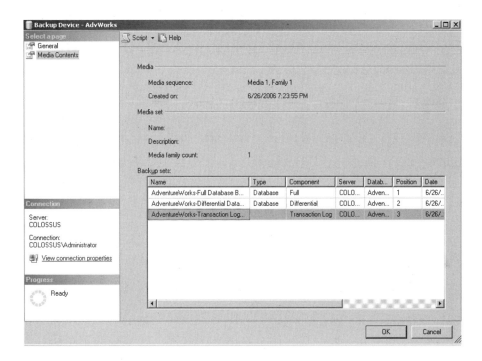

4. Click OK to return to SQL Server Management Studio.

Exercise 17.5	Performing a Filegroup Backup
Scenario	The database you created for your sales department has grown very large—so large that it does not fit on a single disk anymore. To accommodate this growth and enhance performance, you have decided to spread the Sales database across multiple disks using a filegroup. You know that performing a filegroup backup is the fastest backup method for large databases, so you have decided to start performing filegroup backups on Sales after you create the filegroup.
Duration	This task should take approximately 30 minutes.

Setup	For this task, you need access to the machine you installed SQL Server 2005 on in Exercise 2.1, the Sales database you created in Exercise 5.1, and the AdvWorks backup device you created in Exercise 17.1.
Caveat	In a production environment, you would not ordinarily add a new data file to a filegroup on the same disk as the Primary filegroup. The new filegroup would be on a separate disk.
Procedure	In this task, you will create a filegroup for the Sales database, add a table to the new filegroup, and perform a filegroup backup on Sales.
Equipment Used	For this task, you need access to the machine you installed SQL Server 2005 on in Exercise 2.1, the Sales database you created in Exercise 5.1, and the AdvWorks backup device you created in Exercise 17.1.
Objective	To add a filegroup to the Sales database.
Criteria for Completion	This task is complete when you have added a new filegroup to the Sales database, added a table named Employees to the new filegroup, and performed a filegroup backup stored in the AdvWorks backup device.

■ PART A: Creating a Second Filegroup

1. Open SQL Server Management Studio. Expand your server, and then expand Databases.
2. Right-click the Sales database, and select Properties.
3. On the Filegroups page, click the Add button. In the Name text box, enter Secondary.

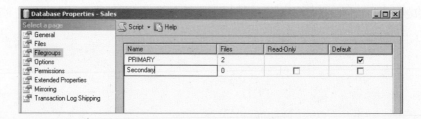

4. On the Files page, click the Add button, and enter this information:
   - Name: Sales_Data3
   - File Type: Data
   - Filegroup: Secondary
   - Initial Size: 3
5. Click OK to create the new file on the Secondary filegroup.

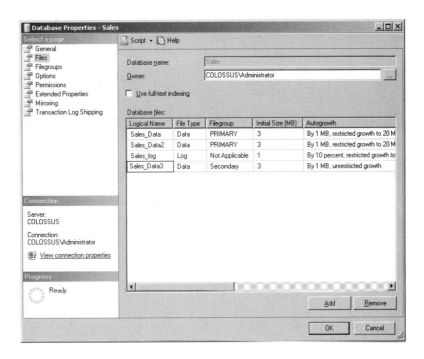

6. Now, to add a table to the new filegroup, expand Sales in Object Explorer, right-click Tables, and select New Table.

7. Under Column Name in the first row, enter Emp_Name.

8. Next to Emp_Name, select varchar as the datatype. Leave the default length of 50.

9. Just below Emp_Name in the second row, enter Emp_Number as the column name with a type of varchar. Leave the default length of 50.

10. Select View Properties Window.

11. Expand the Regular Data Space Specification section, and change the Filegroup or Partition Scheme Name setting to Secondary.

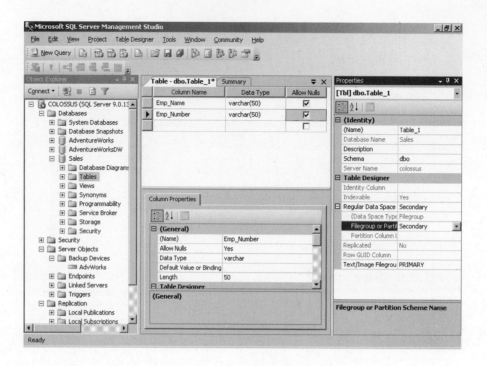

12. Click the Save button (it looks like a floppy disk on the toolbar) to create the new table.

13. Close the table designer by clicking the X in the upper-right corner of the window and enter Employees for the table name.

14. Now, to add some data to the new table, open a new query, and execute the following code (note that the second value is arbitrary):

```
USE Sales INSERT Employees VALUES('Tim Hsu', 'VA1765FR') INSERT Employees
VALUES('Sue Hernandez', 'FQ9187GL')
```

15. Close the query window.

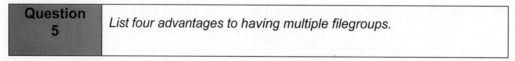

Question 5	List four advantages to having multiple filegroups.

■ PART B: Performing a Filegroup Backup

1. Right-click the Sales database in Object Explorer, point to Tasks, and select Back Up.

2. In the Backup dialog box, make sure Sales is the selected database to back up and Backup Type is Full.

3. Under Backup component, select Files and Filegroups.

4. In the Select Files and Filegroups dialog box, check the box next to Secondary, and click OK (notice that the box next to Sales_Data3 is automatically checked).

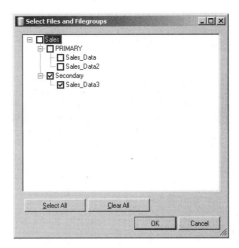

5. Leave the default name in the Name box. In the Description box, enter Filegroup Backup of Sales.
6. Under Destination, make sure the AdvWorks device is the only one listed.

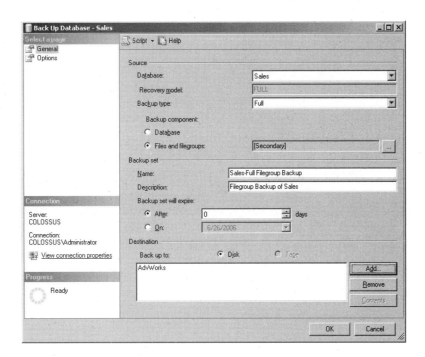

7. On the Options page, make sure Append to the Existing Backup Set is selected so you don't overwrite your existing backups.
8. On the Options page, select Verify Backup When Finished.
9. Click OK to start the backup.
10. When the backup is complete, you will get a notification; click OK to close it.

■ **PART C: Verifying Results**

1. To verify the backup, you can look at the contents of the backup device, so expand Backup Devices under Server Objects in Object Explorer.

2. Right-click AdvWorks, and select Properties.

3. On the Media Contents page, you should see the filegroup backup of Sales.

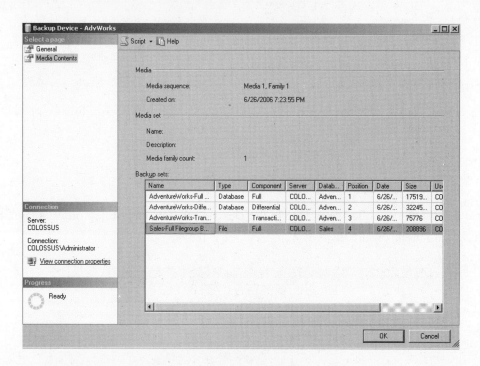

4. Click OK to return to SQL Server Management Studio.

Exercise 17.6	Restoring a Database
Scenario	You have been performing full, differential, and transaction log backups on your databases for some time. Everything was working just fine until this morning; when you came in this morning, the users are complaining that they can't access the database. You try to open the Management Studio but can't; it just won't expand. You know instantly that the database is down and needs to be restored, so you have decided to start the restore process.
Duration	This task should take approximately 30 minutes.
Setup	For this task, you need access to the machine you installed SQL Server 2005 on in Exercise 2.1, the AdventureWorks database installed with the sample data, the AdvWorks backup device you created in Exercise 17.1, the full backup you created in Exercise 17.2, the differential backup you created in Exercise 17.3, and the transaction log backup you created in Exercise 17.4.
Caveat	This task doesn't have any caveats.
Procedure	In this task, you will simulate a downed database by renaming critical files for the AdventureWorks database, and then you will restore the database. You will need to stop all the SQL Server services because while they're running, all the databases are considered open files—you will not be able to work with them outside SQL Server.

Equipment Used	For this task, you need access to the machine you installed SQL Server 2005 on in Exercise 2.1, the AdventureWorks database installed with the sample data, the AdvWorks backup device you created in Exercise 17.1, the full backup you created in Exercise 17.2, the differential backup you created in Exercise 17.3, and the transaction log backup you created in Exercise 17.4.
Objective	To simulate a downed database.
Criteria for Completion	This task is complete when you have taken the AdventureWorks database down and restored it from backup, bringing it back to a usable state.

■ PART A: Retaining Your Original Data

1. Open SQL Server Configuration Manager from the Start menu.
2. In the left pane, select SQL Server 2005 Services.
3. Right-click SQL Server (MSSQLSERVER) in the right pane, and click Stop. You'll be asked whether you want to stop the SQLServerAgent service as well; click Yes.
4. Find the file AdventureWorks_Data.mdf (usually in C:\Program Files\Microsoft SQL Server\MSSQL.1\MSSQL\Data\).
5. Rename the file AdventureWorks_Data.old.
6. Find the file AdventureWorks_Log.ldf, and rename it AdventureWorks_Log.old.
7. From SQL Server Configuration Manager, restart the SQL Agent and SQL Server services.
8. Open SQL Server Management Studio, and expand Databases under your server name. AdventureWorks cannot be expanded and has no summary; it is now inaccessible.

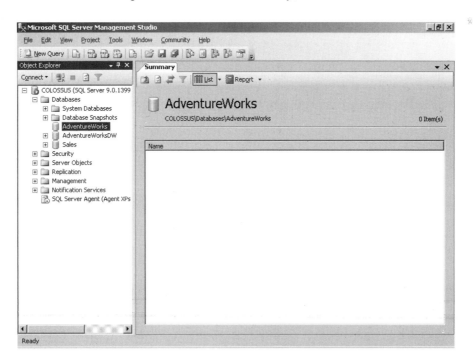

■ PART B: Restoring the Database

1. Right-click Databases, and select Restore Database.
2. In the Restore Database dialog box, select AdventureWorks from the To Database dropdown list box.
3. Under Source for Restore, select From Device. Click the ellipsis (…) button next to the text box to select a device.
4. In the Specify Backup dialog box, select Backup Device from the Backup Media dropdown list box, and click Add.
5. In the Specify Backup dialog box, select AdvWorks, and click OK.

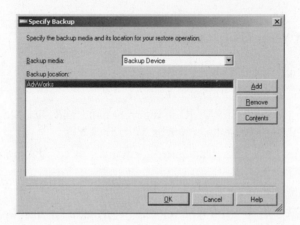

6. Click OK to close the Specify Backup dialog box.
7. Under Select the Backup Sets to Restore, check all three backups (full, differential, and transaction log). Doing so returns the database to the most recent state.

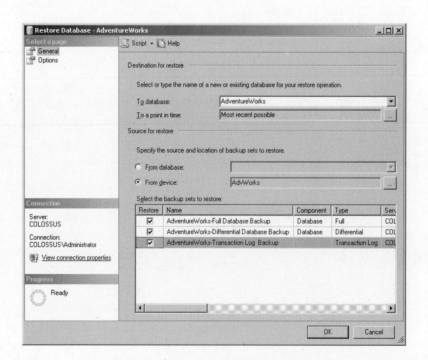

8. On the Options page, make sure the RESTORE WITH RECOVERY option is selected, because you have no more backups to restore.

> **NOTE**
>
> *When a disaster occurs try to backup the tail log first. Restore each backup file in the correct order with NO RECOVERY until the last file when you use WITH RECOVERY. Again, remember to use WITH RECOVERY on only the last media set.*

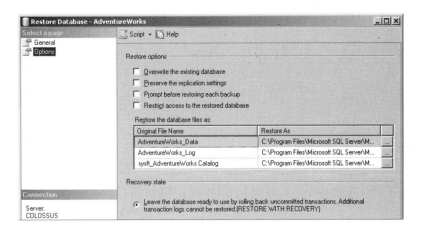

9. Click OK to begin the restore process.
10. Click OK in the dialog box that opens after the restore is complete.

■ PART C: Verifying Results

1. In SQL Server Management Studio, right-click Databases, and click Refresh.
2. Expand Databases, and you should see AdventureWorks is back to normal.

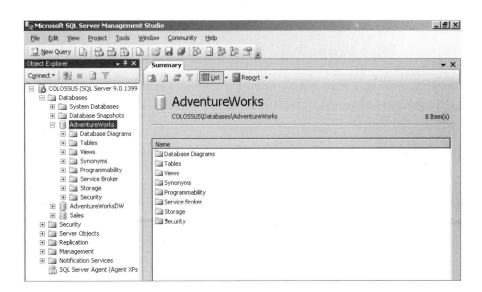

Exercise 17.7	Performing a Point-in-Time Restore
Scenario	It is the end of the month, which is the time when your accounting department performs all its month-end transactions to close the books and bring everything into balance. This has been an especially busy month for your company, so your accounting department has brought in some contract workers to assist with the month-end closeout. One of the contract workers is not familiar with your systems and accidentally enters some incorrect data into the system. Fortunately, your accounting manager caught it early and needs your help to remove the corrupt data from the database. You have decided that the best way to accomplish this task is to perform a point-in-time restore.
Duration	This task should take approximately 30 minutes.
Setup	For this task, you need access to the machine you installed SQL Server 2005 on in Exercise 2.1, the AdventureWorks database installed with the sample data, and the AdvWorks backup device you created in Exercise 17.1.
Caveat	This task doesn't have any caveats.
Procedure	In this task, you will update the HumanResources.Shift table of the AdventureWorks database, wait for two minutes, and update it again. You will then perform a transaction log backup of the database and a subsequent point-in-time restore.
Equipment Used	For this task, you need access to the machine you installed SQL Server 2005 on in Exercise 2.1, the AdventureWorks database installed with the sample data, and the AdvWorks backup device you created in Exercise 17.1.
Objective	To restore your database to a previous known condition.
Criteria for Completion	This task is complete when you have created two new records in the HumanResources.Shift table of the AdventureWorks database and performed a point-in-time restore to eliminate the most recent update.

■ **PART A: Adding Some Records**

1. You need to add a record that will survive the restore. Open a new SQL Server query in SQL Server Management Studio by clicking the New Query button on the toolbar.

2. To create a new record, enter and execute the following code:

```
USE AdventureWorks INSERT HumanResources.Shift(Name, StartTime, EndTime,
ModifiedDate) VALUES('Test Shift 1', getdate() + 1, getdate()+ 2,
getdate())
```

3. Note the time right now.

4. Wait two minutes, clear the query window, and then enter a new record using the following code:

```
USE AdventureWorks INSERT HumanResources.Shift(Name, StartTime, EndTime,
ModifiedDate) VALUES('Test Shift 2', getdate()+1, getdate()+ 2, getdate())
```

5. To see both records, clear the query window, and enter and execute the following code:

```
USE AdventureWorks SELECT * FROM HumanResources.Shift
```

6. Close all open queries.

■ PART B: Performing a Transaction Log Backup

1. To perform a point-in-time restore, you must perform a transaction log backup. In Object Explorer, right-click AdventureWorks, point to Tasks, and select Back Up.

2. In the Backup dialog box, make sure AdventureWorks is the selected database to back up and Backup Type is Transaction Log.

3. Leave the default name in the Name box. In the Description box, enter Point-in-time Backup of AdventureWorks.

4. Under Destination, make sure the AdvWorks device is listed.

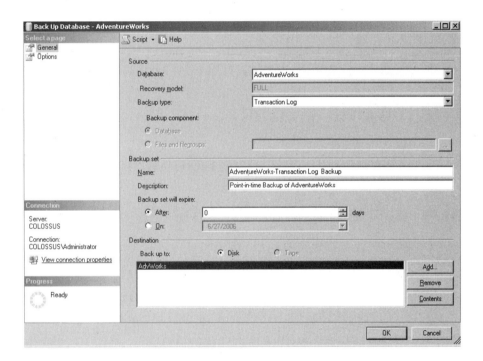

5. On the Options page, make sure Append to the Existing Backup Set is selected so you don't overwrite your existing full backup.

6. On the Options page, select Verify Backup When Finished.

7. Click OK to start the backup.

8. Click OK to close the dialog box that opens when the backup is complete.

9. Now you have to back up the tail of the log, which is all the transactions in the log that have not been backed up or recorded to the data file yet. In Object Explorer, right-click AdventureWorks, point to Tasks, and select Back Up.

10. In the Backup dialog box, make sure AdventureWorks is the selected database to back up and Backup Type is Transaction Log.

11. Leave the default name in the Name box. In the Description box, enter Tail Backup of AdventureWorks.

12. Under Destination, make sure the AdvWorks device is listed.

13. On the Options page, make sure Append to the Existing Backup Set is selected so you don't overwrite your existing full backup.

14. On the Options page, select Verify Backup When Finished.

15. On the Options page, back up the tail of the log.

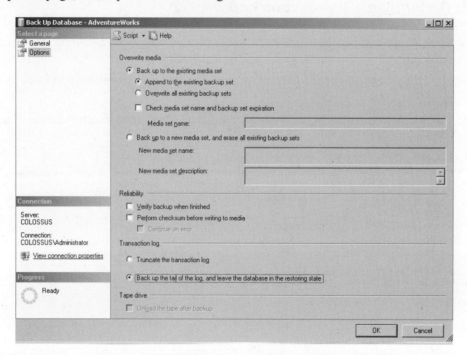

16. Click OK to start the backup.

17. Click OK to close the dialog box that opens when the backup is complete.

■ PART C: Performing a Point-in-Time Restore

1. Open SQL Server Management Studio. Expand your server, and then expand Databases.

2. Right-click AdventureWorks, point to Tasks, move to Restore, and select Database.

3. Click the ellipsis button next to the To a Point in Time text box.

4. In the Point in Time Restore dialog box, enter the time from Step 3 of Part A, Click on the Options tab, select Overwrite the Existing Database, and click OK.

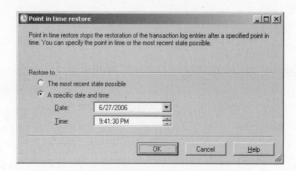

5. Make sure you're restoring from the AdvWorks device, select all the available backups in the device, and click OK to perform the restore.

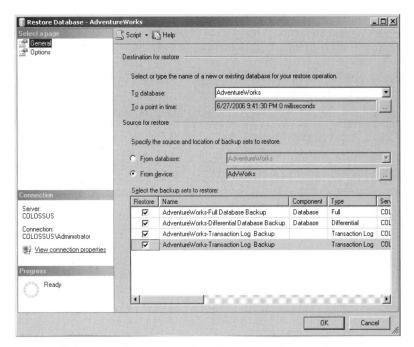

6. Click OK to close the dialog box that opens when the restore is complete.

Question 6	*Can you also perform a restore up to the action of a specific transaction? How?*

■ PART D: Verifying Results

1. Open a new SQL Server Query in SQL Server Management Studio, and enter and execute the following code:

```
USE AdventureWorks SELECT * FROM HumanResources.Shift
```

2. Notice that Test Shift 2 is no longer there, but Test Shift 1 remains.

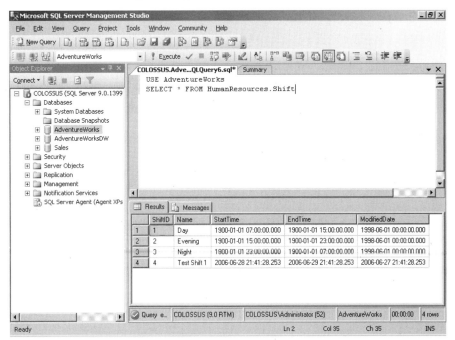

LAB 18
AUTOMATING MAINTENANCE

This lab contains the following exercises and activities:

Exercise 18.1	Configuring Database Mail
Scenario	You work for a medium-sized company that has SQL Server 2005 installations at major offices throughout the country. You need to make sure the systems are up and running at all times, but it is not always easy for you to check the servers' status because they are geographically scattered. You have decided the best way to keep track of your servers is to have them e-mail you when there is a notable status change, such as an error or a completed job. To make that happen, you need to configure the MSDB database as a mailhost database.
Duration	This task should take approximately 30 minutes.
Setup	For this task, you need access to the machine you installed SQL Server 2005 on in Exercise 2.1.

Caveat	This task doesn't have any caveats.
Procedure	In this task, you will configure a mailhost, and then you will configure the SQL Server Agent service to use the mailhost.
Equipment Used	For this task, you need access to the machine you installed SQL Server 2005 on in Exercise 2.1.
Objective	To configure a mailhost.
Criteria for Completion	This task is complete when you have configured a mailhost and configured the SQL Server Agent service to use the mailhost to send mail.

■ PART A: Creating a Mail Profile

NOTE	*You may create a mail profile for both SQL Mail and Database Mail (Database Mail is new to SQL Server 2005). Be sure you know the differences and why you might want to use the newer mail system over the legacy mail system.*

1. Open SQL Server Management Studio, and connect to your server.
2. Expand Management in Object Explorer, right-click Database Mail, and select Configure Database Mail. On the welcome screen, click Next.
3. On the Select Configuration Exercise screen, select Set Up Database Mail by Performing the Following Tasks, and click Next.

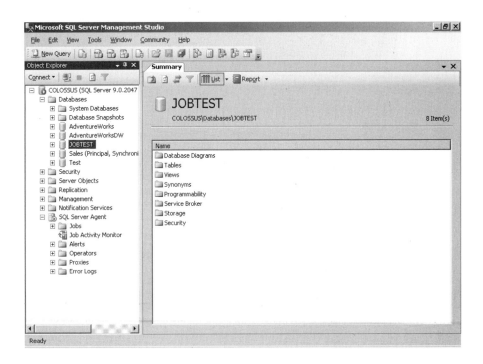

4. If a dialog box opens and asks you whether you would like to enable Database Mail, click Yes.

5. On the New Profile screen, create a mail profile, and associate it with a mail server account:

    a. Enter SQLAgentProfile in the Profile Name box.

    b. Under SMTP Accounts, click Add.

    c. In the Account Name box, enter Mail Provider Account 1.

    d. In the Description box, enter e-mail account information.

    e. Enter your outgoing mail server information using the information provided by your ISP or network administrator.

    f. If your e-mail server requires you to log in, check the Basic Authentication box, and enter your login information.

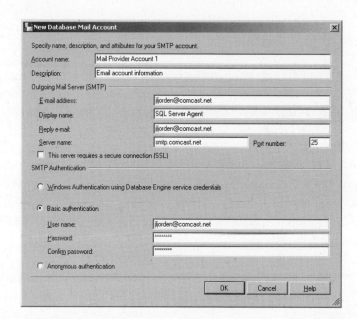

    g. Click OK to return to the wizard. Your account should now be listed under SMTP Accounts.

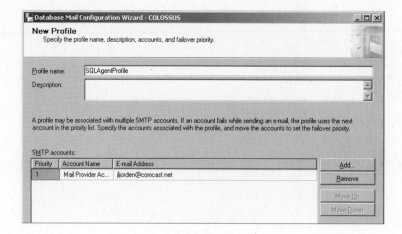

6. Click Next.

7. On the Manage Profile Security screen, check the Public box next to the mail profile you just created to make it accessible to all users. Set the Default Profile option to Yes, and click Next.

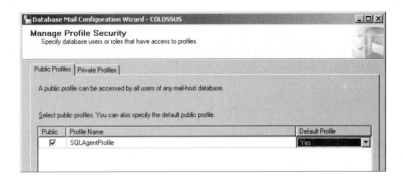

8. On the Configure System Parameters screen, accept the defaults, and click Next.

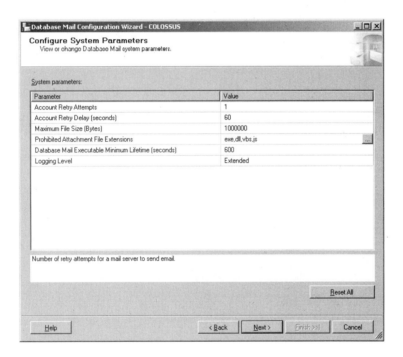

9. On the Complete the Wizard screen, review all your settings, and click Finish.
10. When the system is finished setting up Database Mail, click Close.

■ PART B: Configuring SQL Server Agent

1. In Object Explorer, right-click SQL Server Agent, and select Properties.
2. On the Alert System screen, check the Enable Mail Profile box.
3. Select Database Mail from the Mail System drop-down list.
4. Select SQLAgentProfile from the Mail Profile drop-down list.

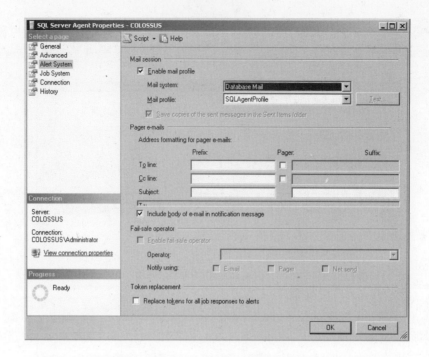

5. Click OK.

6. In Object Explorer, right-click SQL Server Agent, and click Restart.

7. Click Yes in the subsequent dialog box that opens.

■ PART C: Verifying Results

1. Expand Management in Object Explorer, right-click Database Mail, and select Send Test E-mail.

2. Enter your e-mail address in the To text box, and click Send Test E-mail.

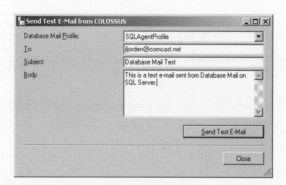

3. Wait for the e-mail to arrive in your inbox. When it arrives, click OK in the dialog box that opens.

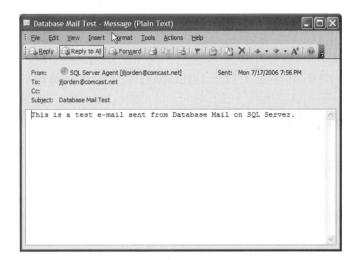

NOTE

Unless Windows Server is configured with the Post Office Protocol (POP-3), this step will fail. POP-3 is not loaded by default. You must insert the Server distribution disk to add and configure the required utilities.

Exercise 18.2	Creating an Operator
Scenario	You work for a medium-sized company that has SQL Server 2005 installations at major offices throughout the country. You are the lead DBA, and you have several assistant DBAs working for you at the remote offices. You need to make sure you are alerted to problems on the servers when they arise and you want to make sure the appropriate assistant DBA is alerted as well, so you have decided to create operators for yourself and your assistants. You also want to make sure coverage exists 24/7, so you have decided to configure yourself as the fail-safe operator.
Duration	This task should take approximately 15 minutes.
Setup	For this task, you need access to the machine you installed SQL Server 2005 on in Exercise 2.1.
Caveat	Make sure the Messenger service is running, or you will not receive Net Send messages.
Procedure	In this task, you will create an operator and configure that operator as the fail-safe operator.
Equipment Used	For this task, you need access to the machine you installed SQL Server 2005 on in Exercise 2.1.
Objective	To create an operator.
Criteria for Completion	This task is complete when you have successfully created an operator and configured the SQL Server Agent to use that operator as the fail-safe operator.

■ PART A: Creating an Operator

1. Open SQL Server Management Studio.

2. In Object Explorer, expand your server, and then expand SQL Server Agent.

3. Right-click Operators, and select New Operator.

4. In the Name box, enter Administrator.

5. If you configured your system to use Database Mail, enter your e-mail address as the e-mail name. If you didn't configure your system to use e-mail, skip this step.

6. Enter the name of your machine in the Net Send Address box. You can find the name by rightclicking the My Computer icon on the Desktop, selecting Properties, and then clicking the Network Identification tab. The computer name is the first section of the full computer name (before the first period). For instance, if the full computer name is instructor.domain.com, the computer name is instructor.

7. If you carry a pager that is capable of receiving e-mail and you've configured Database Mail, you can enter your pager's e-mail address in the Pager E-mail Name box.

8. At the bottom of the page, you can select the days and times this operator is available for notification. If a day is checked, the operator will be notified on that day between the start and end times noted under Start Time and End Time. Check the box for each day, and leave the default workday times of 8:00 A.M. to 6:00 P.M.

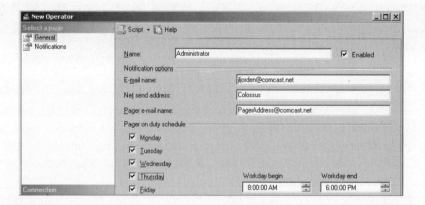

9. Click OK to create the operator.

Question 1	What is a fail-safe operator? How does this operator differ from what you just created?

■ PART B: Configuring SQL Server Agent

1. In SQL Server Management Studio, right-click the SQL Server Agent icon in Object Explorer, and select Properties.

2. On the Alert System screen, check the Enable Fail-Safe Operator box.

3. Select Administrator in the Operator drop-down list.

4. Check the box next to Net Send so you'll receive Net Send messages as a fail-safe operator.

5. Click OK to apply the changes.

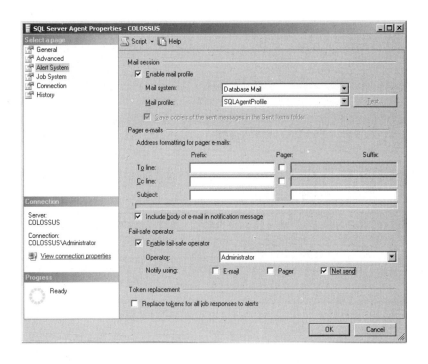

■ PART C: Verifying Results

1. In Object Explorer, expand your server, and then expand SQL Server Agent.
2   Expand Operators; you should see the Administrator operator listed.

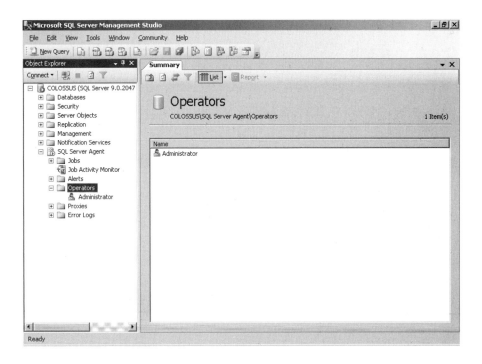

Exercise 18.3	Creating a Job
Scenario	You work for a medium-sized company that has SQL Server 2005 installations at major offices throughout the country. As the lead DBA, it is up to you to make sure maintenance takes place regularly on the databases. You know that the best way to guarantee this is to create jobs to automate the maintenance tasks.
Duration	This task should take approximately 30 minutes.
Setup	For this task, you need access to the machine you installed SQL Server 2005 on in Exercise 2.1 and the operator you created in Exercise 18.2.
Caveat	This database was created in Exercise 14.1. You will need to delete the database in order to complete this exercise.
Procedure	In this task, you'll create a job that builds a database named JobTest and then backs it up.
Equipment Used	For this task, you need access to the machine you installed SQL Server 2005 on in Exercise 2.1 and the operator you created in Exercise 18.2.
Objective	To create a job that builds and backs up a new database.
Criteria for Completion	This task is complete when you have successfully created a job that builds and backs up a database named JobTest.

■ PART A: Creating a Job

Question 2	You can create a job in SQL Server or you can schedule a batch file in the operating system. Both can perform exactly the same functions. Which is preferred? Why?

1. Open SQL Server Management Studio by selecting it from the SQL Server 2005 group under Programs on the Start menu.

2. Expand your server in Object Explorer, and then expand SQL Server Agent.

3. Right-click Jobs, and select New Job.

4. In the Name box, enter Create JobTest Database (leave the rest of the boxes on this screen with the default settings).

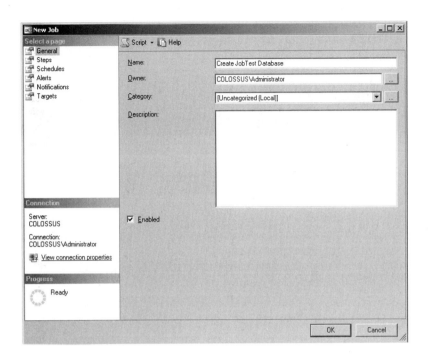

5. Go to the Steps page, and click the New button to create a new step.

6. In the Step Name box, enter Create Database.

7. Leave Type as Transact-SQL, and enter the following code in the Command text box to create a database named JobTest on the C drive:

```
CREATE      DATABASE     JOBTEST     ON      PRIMARY     (NAME=jobtest_dat,
FILENAME='c:\jobtest.mdf', SIZE=10 MB, MAXSIZE=15, FILEGROWTH=10%)
```

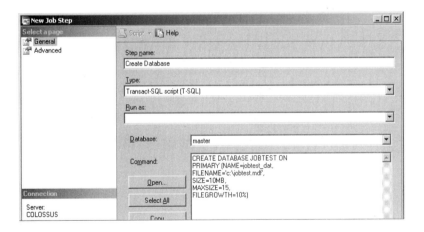

8. Click the Parse button to verify you entered the code correctly, and then move to the Advanced page.

9. On the Advanced page, verify that On Success Action is set to Go to the Next Step and that On Failure Action is set to Quit the Job Reporting Failure. Click OK.

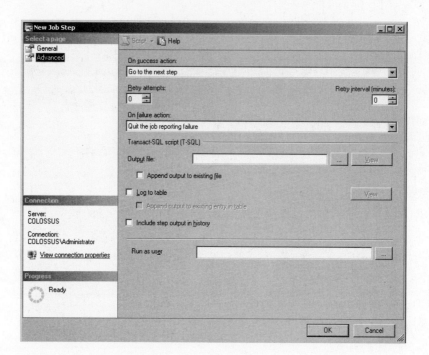

10. To create the second step of the job, click the New button.
11. In the Name box, enter Back Up Test.
12. Leave Type as Transact-SQL Script, and enter the following code in the Command text box to back up the database once it has been created:

```
EXEC  sp_addumpdevice  'disk',  'JobTest_Backup',  'c:\JobTest_Backup.dat'
BACKUP DATABASE JOBTEST TO JobTest_Backup
```

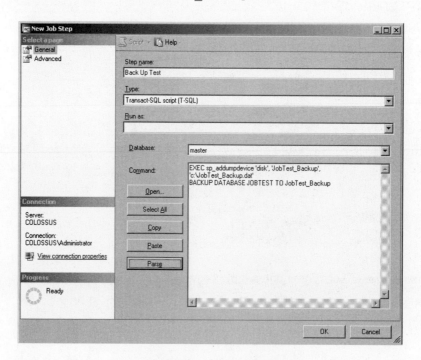

13. Click the Parse button to verify you entered the code correctly.
14. Click OK to create the step; you should now have two steps listed on the Steps page.

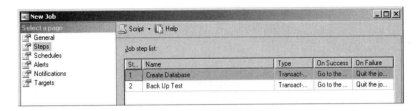

15. Move to the Schedules page, and click the New button to create a schedule that will instruct SQL Server when to fire the job.

16. In the Name box, enter Create and Back Up Database.

17. Select One Time from the Schedule Type drop-down list. Set the time to be five minutes from the time displayed in the system tray (usually at the bottom-right corner of your screen).

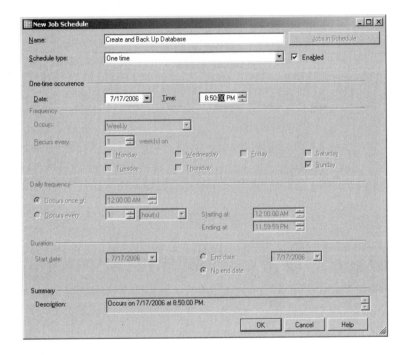

18. Click OK to create the schedule, and move to the Notifications tab.

19. On the Notifications page, check the boxes next to E-mail (if you configured Database Mail earlier) and Net Send, choosing Administrator as the operator to notify. Next to each, select When the Job Completes from the list box (this will notify you no matter what the outcome of the job is).

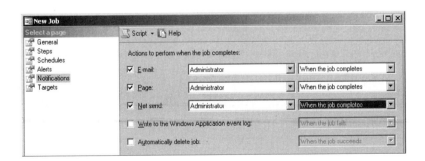

20. Click OK to create the job.

■ PART B: Verifying Results

1. Wait until the time set in Step 17.

2. At that time, you should see a message pop up on your screen, notifying you of completion. You can then check for the existence of the JobTest database in SQL Server Management Studio and the c:\JobTest_Backup.dat file. You should see the JobTest database in Object Explorer after the job runs.

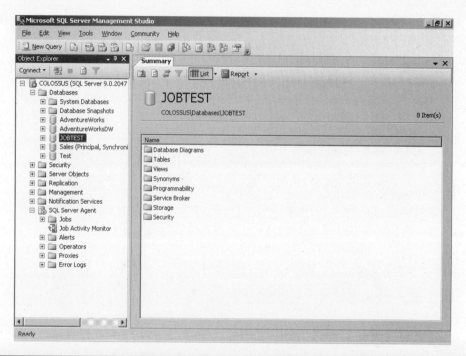

Exercise 18.4	Creating an Alert
Scenario	You have a sales database on your SQL Server that contains customer information. Part of the information stored therein is the customer credit limit. Your sales manager wants to be notified when someone on his team tries to increase a customer's credit limit to greater than $10,000. You know no built-in error message will handle this task, so you decide to create a custom error message and fire it using the RAISERROR() command.
Duration	This task should take approximately 15 minutes.
Setup	For this task, you need access to the machine you installed SQL Server 2005 on in Exercise 2.1 and the operator you created in Exercise 18.2.
Caveat	The Messenger service must be running for you to receive Net Send messages.
Procedure	In this task, you'll create a custom error message that accepts a string parameter and then create an alert based on the custom error message.
Equipment Used	For this task, you need access to the machine you installed SQL Server 2005 on in Exercise 2.1 and the operator you created in Exercise 18.2.
Objective	To create an alert that is based on a custom error message.
Criteria for Completion	This task is complete when you have successfully created an alert based on a custom error message that accepts a string parameter.

■ PART A: Creating an Alert

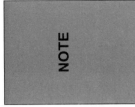

> **NOTE**
>
> *Don't focus on this specific example which only generates an alert message for an undeclared situation but instead work through this exercise thinking about what are good candidate alerts. How about running out of log disk space? How about exceeding 80% CPU usage most of the time?*

1. Open a new SQL Server query by clicking the New Query button in SQL Server Management Studio.

2. Enter and execute the following code to create a new error that is logged to the Windows event log every time it fires:

```
USE master
GO
EXEC sp_addmessage @msgnum=50001, @severity=10, @msgtext=N' This is a
custom error by %ls.', @with_log='TRUE'
GO
```

3. In Object Explorer, expand your server, and then expand SQL Server Agent.

4. Right-click Alerts, and select New Alert.

5. In the Name box, enter Custom Alert.

6. Select the Error Number radio button, and enter 50001 in the Error Number text box.

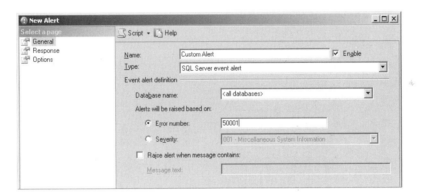

7. On the Response page, check the Notify Operators box, and check the E-mail, Pager, and Net Send boxes next to Administrator.

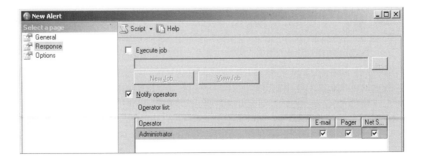

8. On the Options page, check the E-mail, Pager, and Net Send boxes to include the entire text of the error message in the alert, and click OK to create the alert.

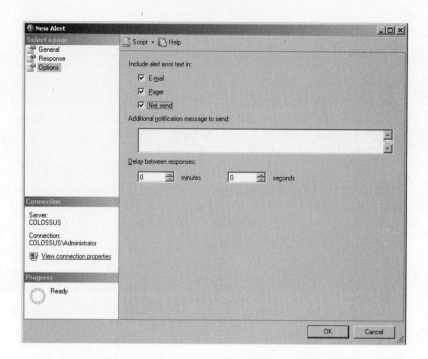

■ PART B: Verifying Results

1. To test the new alert, open a new query, and execute the following code:

    ```
    RAISERROR(50001,10,1,'SQL Guru')
    ```

2. When the e-mail and Net Send message opens, note the detail it gives you, and then click OK.

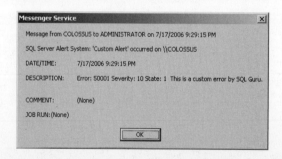

Exercise 18.5	Creating a Database Maintenance Plan
Scenario	As the database administrator for your company, you know how important it is to keep the database system running smoothly at all times. You know quite a few maintenance tasks need to be run regularly to keep the system tuned, such as index reorganizing, database and log backups, file maintenance, and so on. These tasks should be performed during off-peak hours, so you know you need to schedule all these tasks; however, you do not want to create separate jobs for each of these tasks. To make the task easier, you decide to use the Maintenance Plan Wizard.

Duration	This task should take approximately 30 minutes.
Setup	For this task, you need access to the machine you installed SQL Server 2005 on in Exercise 2.1.
Caveat	Make sure you have SQL Server Integration Services (SSIS) running before starting this task.
Procedure	In this task, you'll create a database maintenance plan for all the databases on your server using the Maintenance Plan Wizard.
Equipment Used	For this task, you need access to the machine you installed SQL Server 2005 on in Exercise 2.1.
Objective	To create a database maintenance plan.
Criteria for Completion	This task is complete when you have successfully created a database maintenance plan for all the databases on the default instance of SQL Server using the Maintenance Plan Wizard.

■ PART A: Creating a Database Maintenance Plan

> *Check Books Online for sqlmaint located at Program Files\Microsoft SQL Server\MSSQL.1\MSSQL\Binn. This runs SQL Server 2000 maintenance plans and works from a command prompt and can, thus, be a scheduled batch file. This will be removed from future versions of SQL Server, however.*

1. In SQL Server Management Studio, expand Management, right-click Maintenance Plans, and select Maintenance Plan Wizard.

2. On the welcome screen, click the Next button.

3. On the Select a Target Server screen, enter Maintenance Plan 1 in the Name box, enter a description if you'd like, select your default instance of SQL Server, and click Next.

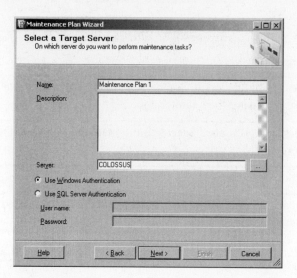

4. On the Select Maintenance Tasks screen, check the boxes for all the available tasks except Execute SQL Server Agent Job, and click Next.

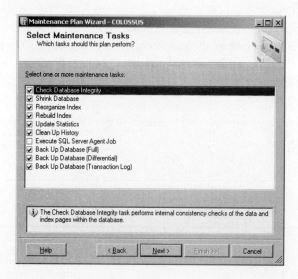

5. On the next screen, you can set the order in which these tasks are performed. Leave the default, and click Next.

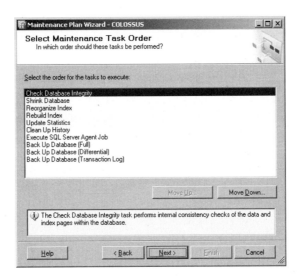

6. The next screen allows you to select the databases on which you want to perform integrity checks. When you click the drop-down list, you'll see several choices:

-   All Databases: This encompasses all databases on the server in the same plan.

-   All System Databases: This choice affects only the master, model, and MSDB databases.

-   All User Databases: This affects all databases (including AdventureWorks) except the system databases.

-   These Databases: This choice allows you to be selective about which databases to include in your plan.

For this task, select All Databases, click OK, and then click Next.

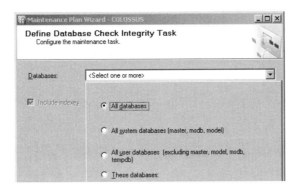

7. On the Define Shrink Database Task screen, select All Databases, click OK, and then click Next.

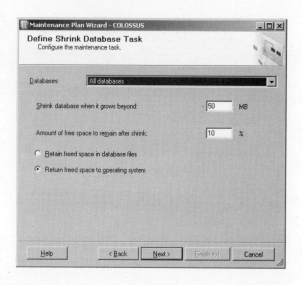

8. On the Define Reorganize Index Task screen, select All Databases from the Databases drop-down list, click OK, and then click Next.

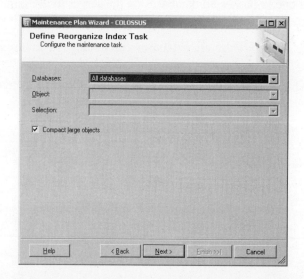

9. The Define Rebuild Index Task screen gives you a number of options for rebuilding your indexes:

   - Reorganize Pages with the Default Amount of Free Space: This regenerates pages with their original fill factor.

   - Change Free Space per Page Percentage To: This creates a new fill factor. If you set this to 10, for example, your pages will contain 10 percent free space.

   Again, select All Databases, accept the defaults, click OK, and then click Next.

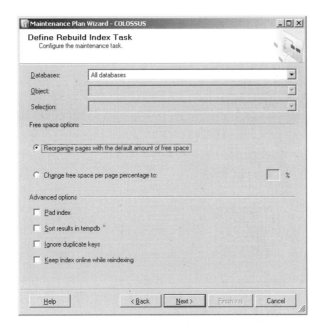

10. Next comes the Define Update Statistics Task screen. Again, select All Databases, click OK, and then click Next.

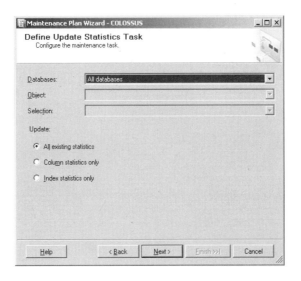

11. Next is the Define History Cleanup Task screen. All the tasks performed by the maintenance plan are logged in the MSDB database. This list is referred to as the history, and it can become quite large if you don't prune it occasionally. On this screen, you can set when and how the history is cleared from the database so you can keep it in check. Again, accept the defaults, and click Next.

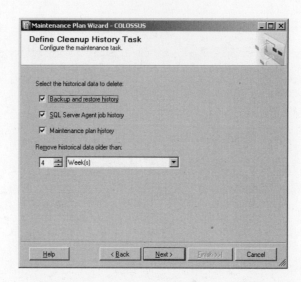

12. The next screen allows you to control how full backups are performed. Select All Databases from the drop-down list, accept the defaults, click OK, and then click Next.

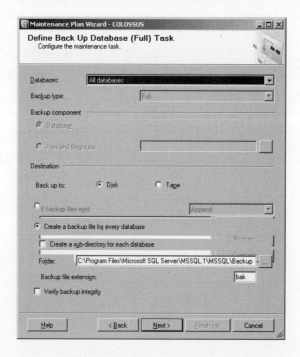

13. The next screen allows you to control how differential backups are performed. Select All Databases from the drop-down list, accept the defaults, click OK, and then click Next.

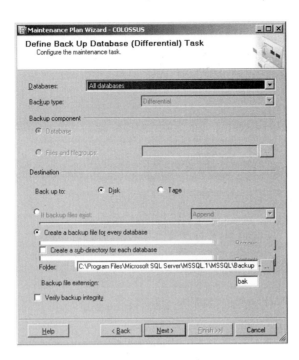

14. The next screen allows you to control how transaction log backups are performed. Select All Databases from the drop-down list, accept the defaults, and click Next.

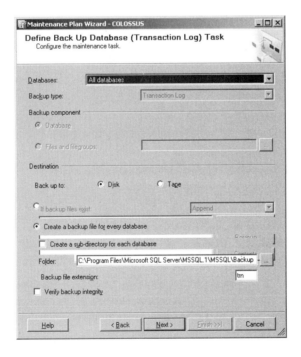

15. On the Select Plan Properties screen, click the Change button to create a schedule for the job.

16. Enter Maintenance Plan 1 Schedule for the schedule name, accept the rest of the defaults, and click OK to create the schedule.

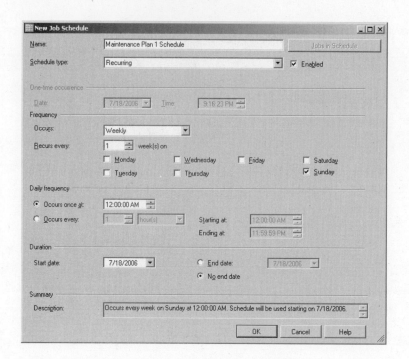

17. Click Next to continue.

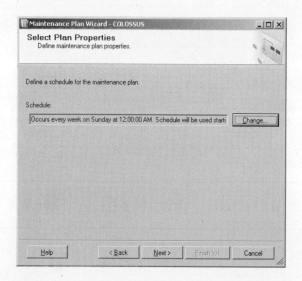

18. On the Select Report Options screen, you can write a report to a text file every time the job runs, and you can e-mail the report to an operator. In this case, write a report to C:\, and click Next.

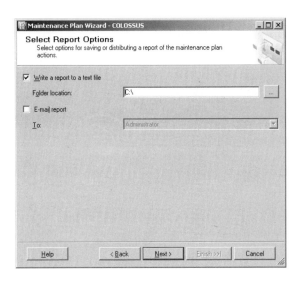

19. On the next screen, you can view a summary of the tasks to perform. Click Finish to create the maintenance plan.

20. Once SQL Server is finished creating the maintenance plan, you can click Close.

Question 3	*You need to run such utilities as backup, DBCC ShrinkFile, DBCC ShrinkDatabase, ALTER DATABASE to compact indexes, and others. If you don't use the Maintenance Wizard what are your options?*

■ PART B: Verifying Results

1. In SQL Server Management Studio, expand Management, and then expand Maintenance Plans. You should see Maintenance Plan 1 listed.

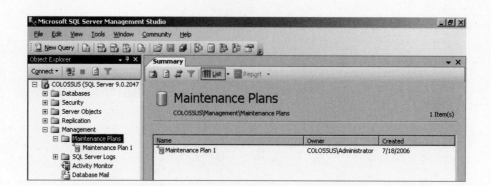

2. Double-click Maintenance Plan 1 to open Design view. You can view and modify all the options you set for the maintenance plan on this screen.

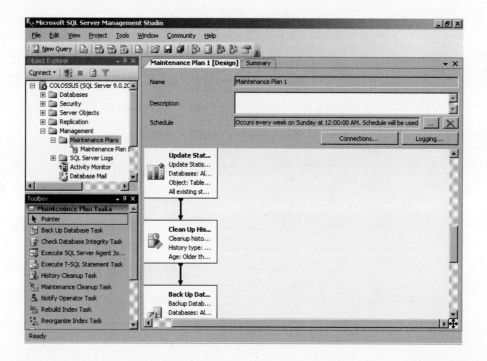

3. Close Design view.

Exercise 18.6	Creating a SQL Server Performance Alert
Scenario	As the lead database administrator (DBA) for your company, you understand how important it is to keep SQL Server up and running at top speed, and you want to make certain that all the databases are available at all times. You have had some trouble with the Sales database, which is heavily used. Occasionally under heavy usage, the transaction log fills to 100 percent, and the users are locked out. You can't find a reliable pattern for when this happens, but you still need to prevent it. You have decided that the best way to keep the log from filling to capacity is to create a performance alert that runs a backup job to clear the log before it gets to 100 percent full.

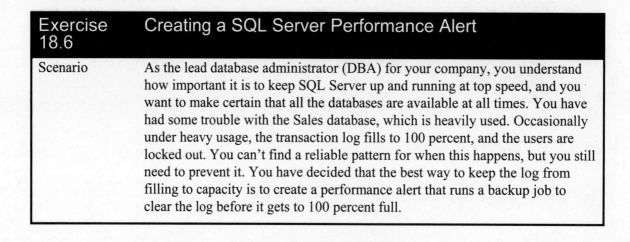

Duration	This task should take approximately 15 minutes.
Setup	For this task, you need access to the machine you installed SQL Server 2005 on in Exercise 2.1, the AdventureWorks database installed with the sample data, and the operator you created in Exercise 18.2.
Caveat	In this task, you will create an alert that fires when the log is less than 100 percent full. On your production systems, you should set such an alert to fire when the log is about 70 percent full and then fire a job that will back up (and thus clear) the transaction log. You will also need to have the Messenger service running to receive the Net Send message.
Procedure	In this task, you'll create an alert that fires when the transaction log for the AdventureWorks database is less than 100 percent full, and you will then disable the alert.
Equipment Used	For this task, you need access to the machine you installed SQL Server 2005 on in Exercise 2.1, the AdventureWorks database installed with the sample data, and the operator you created in Exercise 18.2.
Objective	To create a performance alert in SQL Server Management Studio.
Criteria for Completion	This task is complete when you have created a performance alert that notifies you when the transaction log of the AdventureWorks database is less than 100 percent full.

■ PART A: Creating a SQL Server Performance Alert

1. Open SQL Server Management Studio, expand your server, and then expand SQL Server Agent.
2. Right-click Alerts, and select New Alert.
3. In the Name box, enter Performance Alert.
4. In the Type list, select SQL Server Performance Condition Alert.
5. In the Object box, select SQLServer:Databases.
6. In the Counter box, select Percent Log Used.
7. In the Instance box, select AdventureWorks.
8. Make sure Alert If Counter is set to Falls Below.
9. In the Value box, enter 100.

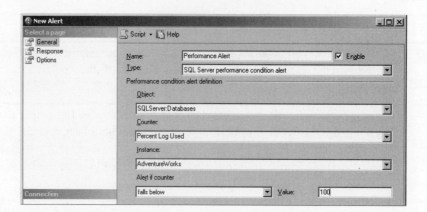

10. Select the Response page, check the Notify Operators box, and check the Net Send box next to your operator name.

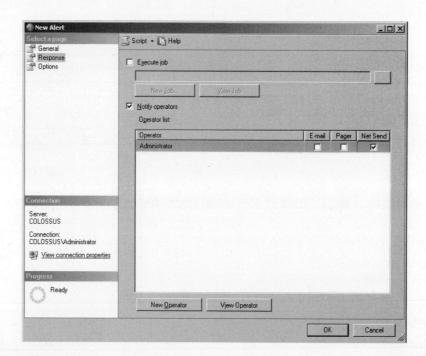

11. Click OK to create the alert.

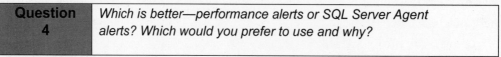

Question 4	Which is better—performance alerts or SQL Server Agent alerts? Which would you prefer to use and why?

12. When the Net Send message opens, note the detail that is provided, and click OK to close the message.

■ PART B: Disabling the Error Message to Prevent It from Popping up Every Few Minutes

1. In SQL Server Management Studio, under Alerts in SQL Server Agent, double-click Performance Alert to expose its properties.
2. Uncheck the Enable box, and click OK to apply the changes.

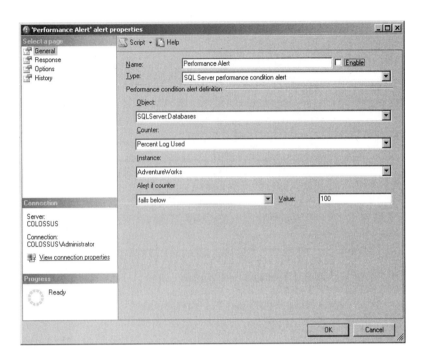

■ PART C: Verifying Results

1. You will see a Net Send message on your screen.

> **NOTE**
>
> *Many administrators disable the messenger service as it is now used by spammers. The resulting messages prove too annoying to allow the beneficial uses.*

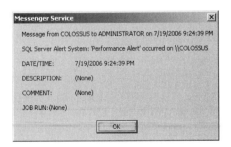

Exercise 18.7	Creating a WMI Alert
Scenario	You are the database administrator (DBA) for a medium-sized company that employs several developers, many of whom create SQL Server objects on a regular basis. Management has implemented a change control program to keep track of what objects are changed and when, and management wants all the developers to follow this new protocol. You have been asked to help make sure no database objects are changed in the production environment without a change control document in place and approved. You could prevent the developers from modifying production objects, but you would have to remove the permissions they need to do their jobs, so you decide to create a WMI alert to notify yourself and management when a production object is modified so you can check for a corresponding change request.
Duration	This task should take approximately 15 minutes.
Setup	For this task, you need access to the machine you installed SQL Server 2005 on in Exercise 2.1 and the operator you created in Exercise 18.2.
Caveat	You must have the Messenger service running to receive the Net Send message.
Procedure	In this task, you will create a WMI alert that fires when a new database is created. You will then disable the alert.
Equipment Used	For this task, you need access to the machine you installed SQL Server 2005 on in Exercise 2.1 and the operator you creatcd in Exercise 18.2.
Objective	To create a Windows Management Instrumentation alert in SQL Server Management Studio.
Criteria for Completion	This task is complete when you have created a performance alert that notifies you when someone has created a new database.

■ PART A: Creating a WMI Alert

1. Open SQL Server Management Studio, expand your server, and then expand SQL Server Agent.
2. Right-click Alerts, and select New Alert.
3. In the Name box, enter WMI Alert.
4. In the Type list, select WMI Event Alert.
5. Make sure Namespace is set to \\.\root\Microsoft\SqlServer\ServerEvents\ MSSQLSERVER.
6. Enter this query in the Query box:

```
SELECT * FROM CREATE_DATABASE
```

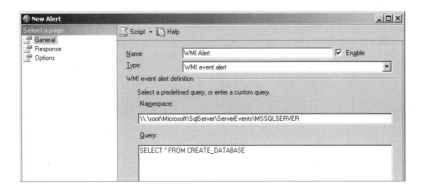

7. Select the Response page, check the Notify Operators box, and check the Net Send box next to your operator name.

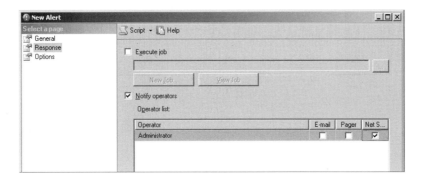

8. On the Options page, check the Net Send box under Include Alert Error Text In, and click OK to create the alert.

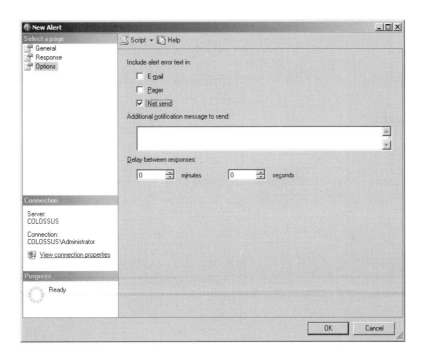

9. Open a new SQL Server query in SQL Server Management Studio by clicking the New Query button.

10. Enter and execute the following code to fire the new alert:

```
USE Master GO CREATE DATABASE WMITest ON PRIMARY ( NAME = N'WMITest',
FILENAME = N'C:\WMITest.mdf' , SIZE = 3072KB , MAXSIZE = UNLIMITED,
FILEGROWTH = 1024KB ) LOG ON ( NAME = N'WMITest_log', FILENAME =
N'C:\WMITest_log.ldf' , SIZE = 504KB , MAXSIZE = UNLIMITED, FILEGROWTH =
10% )
```

11. When the Net Send message opens, note the detail that is provided, and click OK to close the message (it may take a few seconds for the message to open).

12. To disable the alert, open it, uncheck the Enable box, and click OK.

■ PART B: Verifying Results

1. You will see a Net Send message on your screen.

LAB 19
MONITORING AND OPTIMIZING

This lab contains the following exercises and activities:

Exercise 19.1   Using Windows System Monitor

Exercise 19.2   Creating an Alert in Windows System Monitor

Exercise 19.3   Running a Trace in Profiler

Exercise 19.4   Creating a Workload in Profiler

Exercise 19.5   Using the Database Engine Tuning Advisor

Exercise 19.6   Using the Dedicated Administrator Connection

Exercise 19.1	Using Windows System Monitor
Scenario	As the lead database administrator (DBA) for your company, you understand how important it is to keep SQL Server up and running at top speed. You want to make sure all the subsystems on the server are working in harmony and none is being overloaded. The best way to accomplish that goal is to view the data in Windows System Monitor on a regular basis.
Duration	This task should take approximately 15 minutes.
Setup	For this task, you need access to the machine you installed SQL Server 2005 on in Exercise 2.1.
Caveat	This task doesn't have any caveats.
Procedure	In this task, you will work with the graph and report views in Windows System Monitor.

Equipment Used	For this task, you need access to the machine you installed SQL Server 2005 on in Exercise 2.1.
Objective	To work with Windows System Monitor.
Criteria for Completion	This task is complete when you have familiarized yourself with Windows System Monitor.

■ PART A: Using Windows System Monitor

1. Log on to Windows as Administrator.

2. From the Start menu, select Programs, Administrative Tools, and then Performance. Notice that the graph is already populated with counters.

3. On the toolbar, click the Add button (it looks like a + sign) to open the Add Counters dialog box.

4. In the Performance Object box, select Memory.

5. In the Select Counters from List box, select Available Bytes, and click Add.

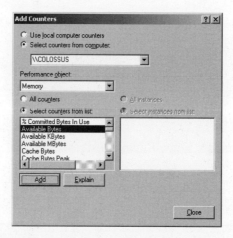

6. Click Close, and notice the graph being created on the screen.

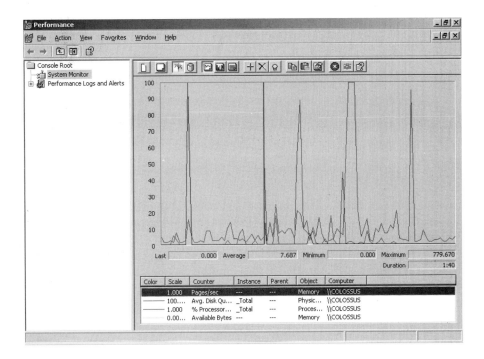

7. Press Ctrl+H, and notice the current counter changes color. This can make the chart easier to read.

8. On the toolbar, click the View Report button (it looks like a sheet of paper), and notice how the same data appears in report view.

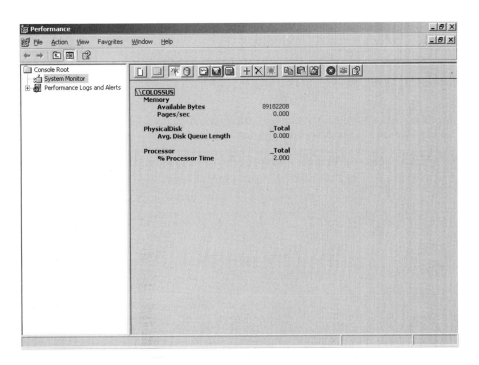

■ **PART B: Verifying Results**

1. Look at each of the other performance objects and counters.

Question 1	Do you understand how each can be used and the importance of each? If not, check Books Online for "Monitoring Resource Usage (System Monitor).

Exercise 19.2	Creating an Alert in Windows System Monitor
Scenario	As the lead database administrator (DBA) for your company, you understand how important it is to keep SQL Server up and running at top speed. You want to make sure all the subsystems on the server are working in harmony and none is being overloaded. The best way to accomplish that goal is to view the data in Windows System Monitor on a regular basis. You need to be notified if a subsystem suddenly becomes overloaded as well, so you decide to create some alerts in Windows System Monitor to keep you updated.
Duration	This task should take approximately 15 minutes.
Setup	For this task, you need access to the machine you installed SQL Server 2005 on in Exercise 2.1.
Caveat	In this task, you will create an alert that notifies you when the Processor:% Processor Time counter is less than 70 percent (which is just an arbitrary value that we use in this task). In production, this would be more than 75 percent.
Procedure	In this task, you will create an alert in Windows System Monitor.
Equipment Used	For this task, you need access to the machine you installed SQL Server 2005 on in Exercise 2.1.
Objective	To work with Windows System Monitor.
Criteria for Completion	This task is complete when you have created an alert that notifies you when the Processor:% Processor Time counter is less than 70 percent, which you should see in Event Viewer as outlined in the earlier task details.

■ **PART A: Creating an Alert in Windows System Monitor**

1. Log on to Windows as Administrator.
2. From the Start menu, select Programs, Administrative Tools, and then Performance.
3. In the left pane, expand Performance Logs and Alerts, right-click Alerts, and select New Alert Settings.
4. Enter Test Alert in the Name box, and click OK.
5. In the Alert Settings dialog box, enter Test Alert in the Comment field.
6. Click Add.
7. Select the Processor object and the % Processor Time counter, and click Add; then click Close.

Question 2	*How many objects and counters can you use to create alerts?*

8. Select Under from the Alert When Value Is drop-down list, enter 70 for Limit, and click OK. This will generate an alert if the processor is not busy 70 percent of the time. In the real world, you would set this to more than 70 percent, thus warning you just before it becomes a serious problem.

9. Click OK to create the alert.

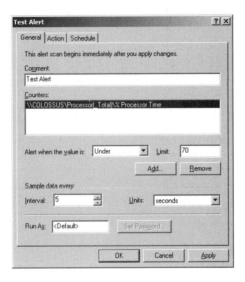

■ PART B: Verifying Results

1. To view the alerts, open Event Viewer, and look for them in the Application log.

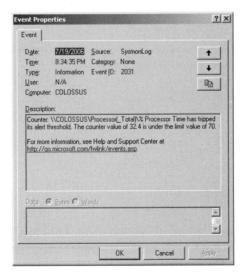

2. Watch the alerts generated for a short time, and then select the alert, and finally press the Delete key. If asked whether you want to continue deleting a running alert, click OK.

3. Exit System Monitor and Event Viewer.

Exercise 19.3	Running a Trace in Profiler
Scenario	You are the database administrator (DBA) for a medium-sized company with several SQL Server users. Recently your users have started complaining that they are having trouble retrieving data from SQL Server. Some users cannot access the data they need at all, and others can access it, but it is slow. You realize that this could be any number of problems ranging from network connectivity to security issues. It could even be a combination of these problems. You realize that the best way to troubleshoot this problem is to run a trace in Profiler.
Duration	This task should take approximately 15 minutes.
Setup	For this task, you need access to the machine you installed SQL Server 2005 on in Exercise 2.1 and the AdventureWorks database installed with the sample data.
Caveat	This task doesn't have any caveats.
Procedure	In this task, you will configure and run a trace in Profiler.
Equipment Used	For this task, you need access to the machine you installed SQL Server 2005 on in Exercise 2.1 and the AdventureWorks database installed with the sample data.
Objective	To create and run a trace in Profiler.
Criteria for Completion	This task is complete when you have created and run a trace in Profiler.

■ PART A: Running a Trace in Profiler

1. From the Start menu, select All Programs, Microsoft SQL Server 2005, Performance Tools, and then SQL Server Profiler.

2. From the File menu, select New Trace.

3. Connect to your default server instance using the proper authentication; this opens the Trace Properties dialog box.

4. In the Trace Name box, enter Monitor.

5. Use the Standard (default) template.

6. Check the Save to File box, and click Save to accept the default name and location. Leave the Enable File Rollover box checked and the Server Processes Trace Data box unchecked.

7. Check the Save to Table box, log on to your default server instance, and fill in the following:
   - Database:AdventureWorks
   - Owner:dbo
   - Table:Monitor

8. Click OK once you have made these changes.

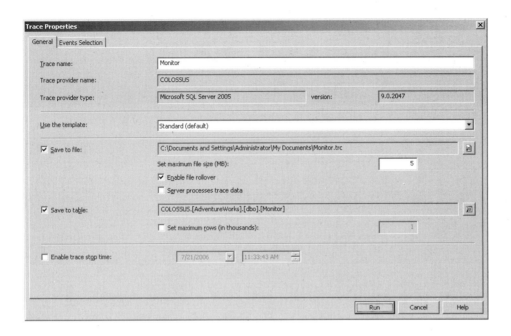

9. Click the Events Selection tab, and check the Show All Events box toward the bottom of the tab.

10. In the Events grid, expand Security Audit (if it is not already expanded), and check the box to the left of Audit Schema Object Access Event. This will monitor the opening and closing of objects, such as tables.

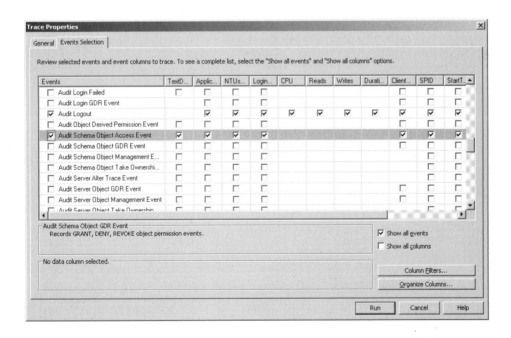

11. Click Run to start the trace.

12. Leave Profiler running, and open a new SQL Server query in SQL Server Management Studio.

13. Execute the following query:

```
USE AdventureWorks SELECT * FROM Person.Contact
```

14. Switch to Profiler, and click the Pause button (double blue lines). In Profiler, notice the amount of data that was collected.

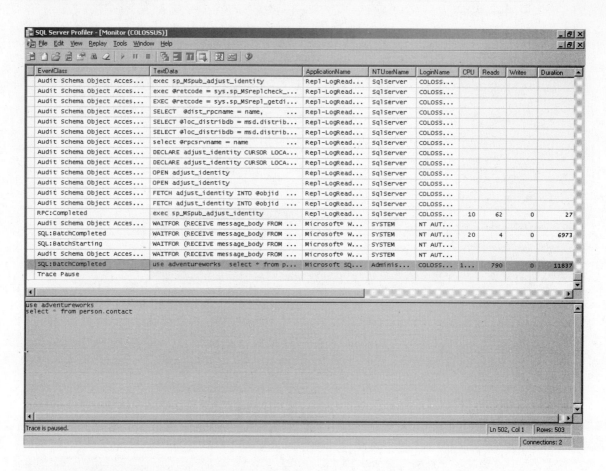

15. Click the Stop button (the red box) to stop the trace.
16. Close Profiler and SQL Server Management Studio.

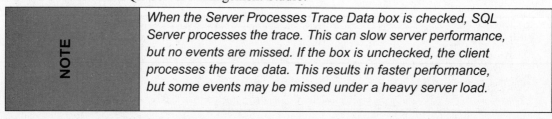

NOTE: When the Server Processes Trace Data box is checked, SQL Server processes the trace. This can slow server performance, but no events are missed. If the box is unchecked, the client processes the trace data. This results in faster performance, but some events may be missed under a heavy server load.

■ PART B: Verifying Results

1. You should see a list of database activity in the task details.

Exercise 19.4	Creating a Workload in Profiler
Scenario	You have a SQL Server 2005 instance that has been running well for several months. Over the past couple of weeks, though, users have started complaining about performance. They tell you that queries are taking an excessive amount of time to return data. After doing some research into the problem, you realize the users have begun to query on columns that are not indexed, and some of the indexes currently in place may not be used any longer. You know that the most efficient way to fix this problem is by using the Database Engine Tuning Advisor; however, before you can do that, you need to create a workload file.
Duration	This task should take approximately 15 minutes.
Setup	For this task, you need access to the machine you installed SQL Server 2005 on in Exercise 2.1, the AdventureWorks database installed with the sample data, and the Monitor table you created in Exercise 19.3.
Caveat	This task doesn't have any caveats.
Procedure	In this task, you will create a workload file by configuring a trace in Profiler based on the Tuning trace template.
Equipment Used	For this task, you need access to the machine you installed SQL Server 2005 on in Exercise 2.1, the AdventureWorks database installed with the sample data, and the Monitor table you created in Exercise 19.3.
Objective	To create a workload in Profiler.
Criteria for Completion	This task is complete when you have created a workload file in Profiler.

■ PART A: Creating a Workload in Profiler

> **NOTE** In a production environment you would run suspect conditions in Profiler during a typical interval (perhaps two weeks) to capture actual user workloads. This exercise manufactures a problem that can be expeditiously repaired.

1. First you need to remove the indexes from the test table, so open SQL Server Management Studio, and expand Databases, AdventureWorks and then Tables.
2. Right-click Monitor, and select Modify.
3. Right-click the key icon by the RowNumber column, and select Remove Primary Key.
4. Click the Save button on the toolbar to remove the indexes from the table.

5. To stop any excess traffic on the server, right-click SQL Server Agent in Object Explorer, select Stop, then click Yes or No.

6. From the Start menu, select Programs, Microsoft SQL Server 2005, Performance Tools, and then Profiler.

7. From the File menu, select New Trace to open the Trace Properties dialog box.

8. Connect to your default server instance using the proper authentication.

9. In the Trace Name box, enter Tuning.

10. Use the Tuning template.

11. Check the Save to File box, and click Save to accept the default name and location. Leave the Enable File Rollover box checked and the Server Processes Trace Data box unchecked.

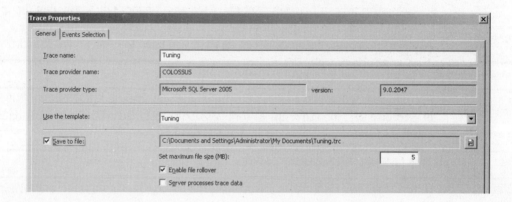

12. Click Run to start the trace.

13. Leave Profiler running, and open a new SQL Server query in SQL Server Management Studio.

14. Execute the following query (make sure to insert your username in the WHERE clause):

```
USE AdventureWorks SELECT textdata FROM monitor WHERE NTUserName =
'<YourUserName>'
```

15. Switch to Profiler, click the Stop button (red box), and then close Profiler.

■ PART B: Verifying Results

1. You should see a list of database activity.

Question 3	What tools can you use to identify suspect conditions to avoid the overhead of monitoring everything?

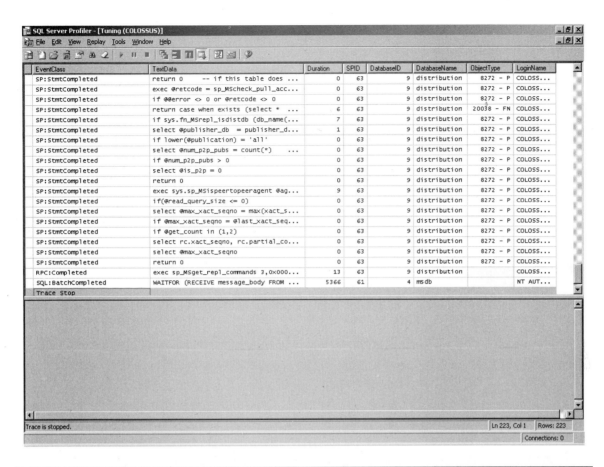

Exercise 19.5	Using the Database Engine Tuning Advisor
Scenario	You have a SQL Server 2005 instance that has been running well for several months. Over the past couple of weeks, though, users have started complaining about performance. They tell you queries are taking an excessive amount of time to return data. After doing some research into the problem, you realize that the users have begun to query on columns that are not indexed, and some of the indexes currently in place may not be used any longer. Because you have already created a workload file, you are ready to tune the database using the Database Engine Tuning Advisor.
Duration	This task should take approximately 15 minutes.
Setup	For this task, you need access to the machine you installed SQL Server 2005 on in Exercise 2.1, the AdventureWorks database installed with the sample data, the Monitor table you created in Exercise 19.3, and the workload file you created in Exercise 19.4.
Caveat	This task doesn't have any caveats.
Procedure	In this task, you will tune the AdventureWorks database using the Database Engine Tuning Advisor and the workload file you created in Exercise 19.4.

Equipment Used	For this task, you need access to the machine you installed SQL Server 2005 on in Exercise 2.1, the AdventureWorks database installed with the sample data, the Monitor table you created in Exercise 19.3, and the workload file you created in Exercise 19.4.
Objective	To run the Database Engine Tuning Advisor.
Criteria for Completion	This task is complete when you have used the Database Engine Tuning Advisor to create an index on the Monitor table in the AdventureWorks database using the Tuning.trc workload file created in Exercise 19.4. You should see a new index on the Monitor table.

■ PART A: Using the Database Engine Tuning Advisor

1. From the Start menu, select All Programs, Microsoft SQL Server 2005, Performance Tools, and then the Database Engine Tuning Advisor.

2. Connect to your server using the appropriate authentication method. This will create a new session in the advisor.

3. In the Session Name box, enter Tuning Session.

4. In the Workload section, click the Browse button (it looks like a pair of binoculars), and locate the Tuning.trc trace file created earlier.

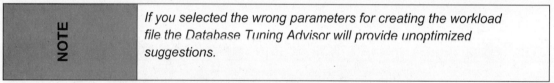

NOTE
If you selected the wrong parameters for creating the workload file the Database Tuning Advisor will provide unoptimized suggestions.

5. In the databases and tables grid, check the box next to AdventureWorks.

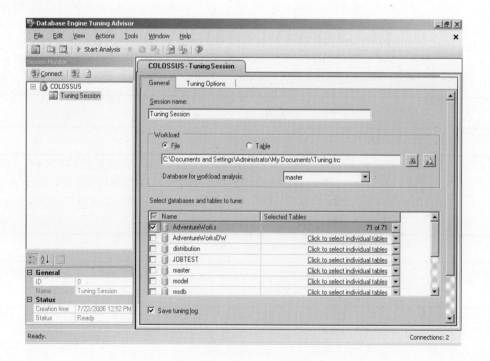

6. Switch to the Tuning Options tab. From here you can instruct the advisor what physical changes to make to the database; specifically, you can have the advisor create new indexes (clustered and nonclustered) and partition the database.

7. Leave the Limit Tuning Time option checked and set for the default time; this prevents the advisor from taking too many system resources.

8. Leave the default options for Physical Design Structures (PDS) to Use in Database, Partitioning Strategy to Employ, and Physical Design Structures (PDS) to Keep in Database.

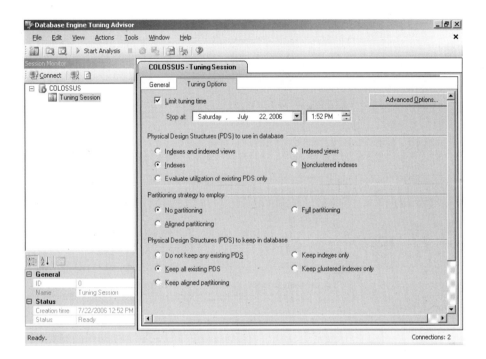

9. Click the Advanced Options button. From here you can set these options:

    *   Define Max. Space for Recommendations (MB) will set the maximum amount of space used by the recommended physical performance structures.

    *   All Recommendations Are Offline will generate recommendations that may require you to take the database offline to implement the change.

    *   Generate Online Recommendations Where Possible will return online recommendations even if a faster offline method is possible. If there is no online method, then an offline method is recommended.

    *   Generate Only Online Recommendations will return only online recommendations.

10. Click Cancel to return to the advisor.

11. Click the Start Analysis button on the toolbar.

12. You should see a progress status screen during the analysis phase.

13. After analysis is complete, you will be taken to the Recommendations tab; you should see a recommendation for creating an index on the Monitor table.

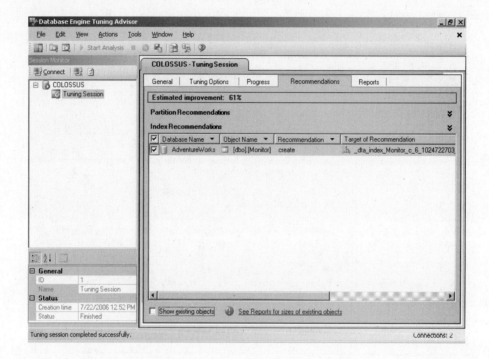

14. You can also check the Reports tab for more detailed information about the analysis process. Select Statement Detail Report from the Select Report drop-down list as an example.

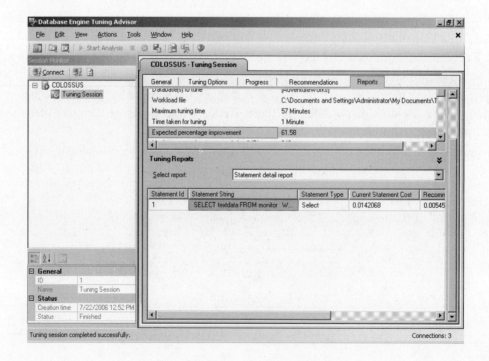

15. To apply these recommendations, select Apply Recommendations from the Actions menu.

16. In the dialog box that opens, click Apply Now, and click OK.

17. When the index has been created, click Close.

18. Close the Database Engine Tuning Advisor.

■ PART B: Verifying Results

1. Open SQL Server Management Studio, expand your server, and then select Databases, AdventureWorks, Tables, Monitor, Indexes.

2. You should see a new index listed.

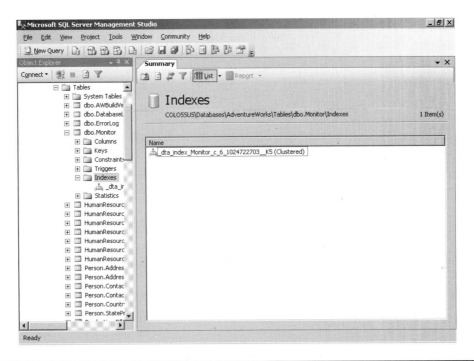

Exercise 19.6	Using the Dedicated Administrator Connection
Scenario	You have a SQL Server 2005 instance that has been running well for several months. Just this morning, though, your developers pushed some new stored procedures into production. A few hours later, users started complaining that they could not connect to SQL Server to retrieve data. While trying to investigate the problem, you find that you cannot connect to SQL Server using SQL Server Management Studio either. You know that the only method left for troubleshooting is the DAC.
Duration	This task should take approximately 15 minutes.
Setup	For this task, you need access to the machine you installed SQL Server 2005 on in Exercise 2.1.
Caveat	This task doesn't have any caveats.

Procedure	In this task, you will connect to the DAC and run a query.
Equipment Used	For this task, you need access to the machine you installed SQL Server 2005 on in Exercise 2.1.
Objective	To connect to the DAC and run a query.
Criteria for Completion	This task is complete when you have connected to the DAC using both the command line and SQL Server Management Studio.

■ PART A: Using the Dedicated Administrator Connection

> **NOTE**
> *This is the only way you can access the RESOURCE hidden database.*

1. Open a command prompt on your server.

2. The following command connects to the server specified with the -S parameter using a trusted connection as specified by the -E parameter. The -A parameter specifies the DAC, or an administrative connection. Run the following command now:

```
Sqlcmd -S (local) -A -E
```

> **NOTE**
> *This works for database repair only if the SQL Server service is running; if not restart the service with sqlservr -m. Check BOL for further details.*

3. You should see a 1> prompt. From here you can enter a query. Type the following, and hit Enter:

```
SELECT session_id, status, blocking_session_id FROM sys.dm_exec_requests
```

4. You should now see a 2> prompt. Type GO, and hit Enter to execute the query.

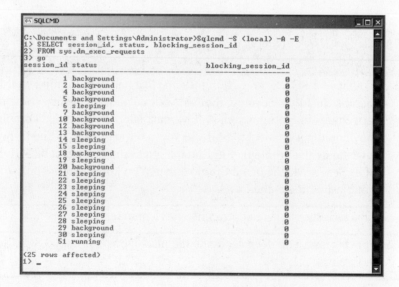

5. You should now be back at the 1> prompt. To exit the DAC, enter EXIT, and hit Enter.

6. To connect to the DAC in SQL Server Management Studio, close all open copies of SQL Server Management Studio.

7. Open SQL Server Management Studio, connect to the default instance, and open a new query.

8. From the Query menu, hover over Connection, and click Change Connection.

9. To connect to the local machine, enter ADMIN: in front of the server name in the Server Name text box, and click Connect.

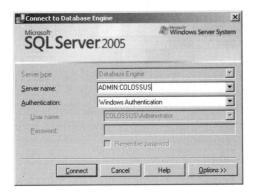

10. Execute this query in the new query window:

```
SELECT session_id, status, blocking_session_id FROM sys.dm_exec_requests
```

11. You should see a list of sessions in the results grid.

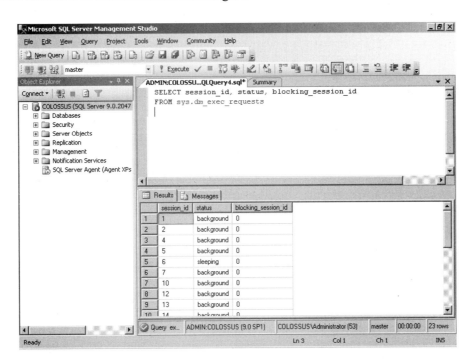

12. Close SQL Server Management Studio.

■ PART B: Verifying Results

1. You should see results from each query as outlined in the PART A of this task.

LAB 20
WORKING WITH HIGH-AVAILABILITY METHODS

This lab contains the following exercises and activities:

Exercise 20.1   Implementing Database Mirroring

Exercise 20.2   Implementing Log Shipping

Exercise 20.3   Creating a Database Snapshot

Exercise 20.4   Reverting from a Database Snapshot

Exercise 20.1	Implementing Database Mirroring
Scenario	You created a database for your sales department several months ago, and your sales staff has started to rely on it quite heavily. In fact, if the database were to go down, your sales managers have told you that their staff would not be able to get their work done. This means lost sales, lost productivity, and possibly even lost customers. This is not something you can let happen; you know that the database must be available to your sales staff at all times because the sales representatives make sales calls at all hours of the day and night. To ensure that the database is always available, you decide to implement a high-safety database mirror.
Duration	This task should take approximately 60 minutes.
Setup	For this task, you need access to the machine you installed SQL Server 2005 on in Exercise 2.1, the second instance of SQL Server 2005 you installed in Exercise 2.2, and the Sales database you created in Exercise 5.1. You will also need to make sure you install SQL Server 2005 Service Pack 1 before performing this task or be prepared to use the correct trace flag.

Caveat	You must have SQL Server 2005 Service Pack 1 installed to use database mirroring or understand the workaround.
Procedure	In this task, you will make a backup of the Sales database and then restore it to the Second instance of SQL Server in the RECOVERY state. You will then create a high-safety database mirror of the Sales database on the Second instance.
Equipment Used	For this task, you need access to the machine you installed SQL Server 2005 on in Exercise 2.1, the Second instance of SQL Server 2005 you installed in Exercise 2.2, and the Sales database you created in Exercise 5.1.
Objective	To implement database mirroring one of the three configurations of database mirroring.
Criteria for Completion	This task is complete when you have successfully mirrored the Sales database from the default instance on your machine to the Second instance.

■ PART A: Backing up the Sales Database from the Default Instance

1. Open SQL Server Management Studio, expand Databases, right-click Sales, point to Tasks, and click Back Up.
2. In the Backup dialog box, make sure Sales is the selected database to back up and Backup Type is Full.
3. Leave the default name in the Name box. In the Description box, enter Full Backup of Sales.
4. Under Destination, a disk device may already be listed. If so, select the device, and click Remove.
5. Under Destination, click Add.
6. In the Select Backup Destination box, click File Name, and in the text box enter x:\temp\Sales.bak (make sure the temp directory exists on the selected drive). Click OK.

7. Click OK to start the backup.
8. When the backup is complete, you will get a notification; click OK to close it.

■ PART B: Backing up the Transaction Log

1. Open SQL Server Management Studio, expand Databases, right-click Sales, point to Tasks, and click Back Up.

2. In the Backup dialog box, make sure Sales is the selected database to back up and Backup Type is Transaction Log.

3. Leave the default name in the Name box. In the Description box, enter Transaction Log Backup of Sales.

4. Make sure x:\temp\Sales.bak is the only device listed, and click OK.

5. Click OK to start the backup.

6. When the backup is complete, you will get a notification; click OK to close it.

■ PART C: Restoring the Database to the Second Instance

> **NOTE**
>
> *In a production environment, you need two servers each with a licensed copy of SQL Server and each must be the same edition: standard-to-standard or enterprise-to-enterprise. A witness server also requires a copy of SQL Server, which can be another production server or even Express Edition running on a workstation.*

1. Open SQL Server Management Studio, and connect to the Second instance by selecting <YourServerName>\SECOND from the Server Name drop-down list. One way to get here is by clicking Connect in your Object Explore. The Connect to Server dialog box appears. Choose Database Engine, then Server name.

2. Right-click Databases, and select Restore Database.

3. Enter Sales in the To Database box.

4. Under Source for Restore, select From Device. Click the ellipsis (...) button next to the text box to select a device.

5. In the Specify Backup dialog box, select File from the Backup Media drop-down list box, and click Add.

6. In the Locate Backup File dialog box, find the Sales.bak file, and click OK.

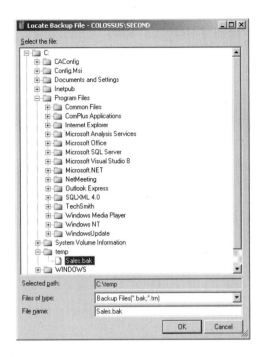

7. Click OK to close the Specify Backup dialog box.

8. Under Select the Backup Sets to Restore, check the boxes for both backups of Sales.

9. On the Options page, in the Restore the Database Files As grid, under the Restore As column, make these changes:

   - Change Sales_data.mdf to Sales_data_mir.mdf.

   - Change Sales_data2.ndf to Sales_data_mir2.ndf.

   - Change Sales_data3.ndf to Sales_data_mir3.ndf.

   - Change Sales_log.ldf to Sales_log_mir.ldf.

10. Also on the Options page, make sure the RESTORE WITH NORECOVERY option is selected.

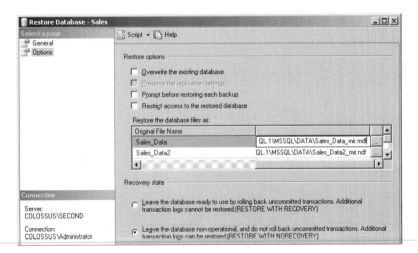

11. Click OK to begin the restore process.

12. Click OK in the dialog box that opens after the restore is complete.

■ PART D: Configuring Database Mirroring

1. Open SQL Server Management Studio, and connect to the default instance.

2. Expand Databases, right-click Sales, point to Tasks, and click Mirror.

3. Click the Configure Security button to start the Configure Database Mirroring Security Wizard, which will create the endpoints required for mirroring.

4. On the welcome screen, click Next.

5. Select No on the Include Witness Server screen, and then click Next.

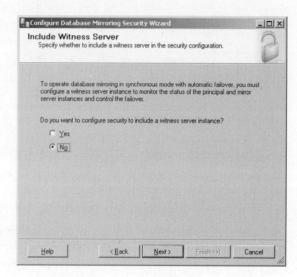

6. On the Choose Servers to Configure screen, click Next.

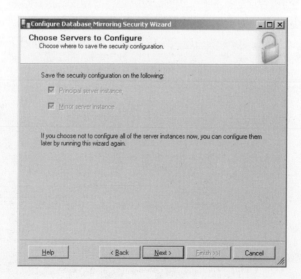

7. On the Principal Server Instance screen, accept the defaults, and click Next.

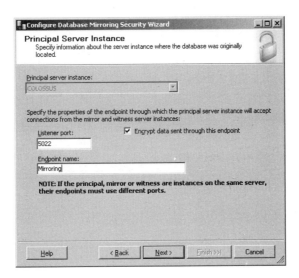

8. On the Mirror Server Instance screen, select the Second instance of SQL Server, and click the Connect button. Then click Connect.

9. Accept the defaults that are filled in for you, and click Next.

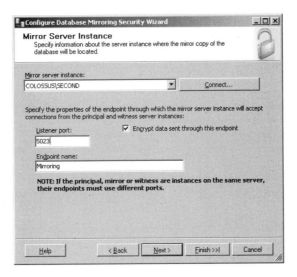

10. On the Service Accounts screen, leave both account names blank because you configured the services to use the same accounts. Click Next.

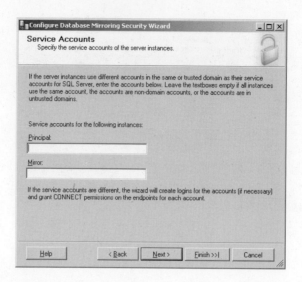

11. On the Complete the Wizard screen, click Finish.

12. Click Close when the wizard is complete.

13. In the Database Properties dialog box that opens, click Start Mirroring.

14. Click OK to close the Database Properties dialog box.

Question 1	How quickly can the mirror respond to users after the production server fails? Compare with restoring from a full backup to a cold standby server. How quickly can you restore services to users without mirroring?

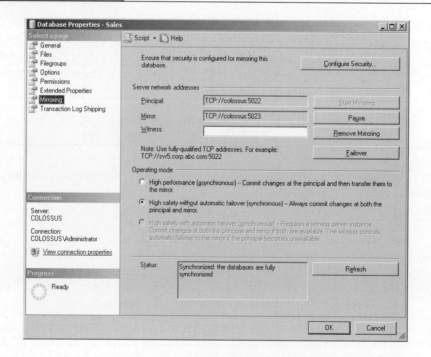

■ PART E: Verifying Results

1. Connect to both instances and look at the Sales database in Object Explorer.

2. On the default instance, you should see (Principal, Synchronized) next to the Sales database.

3 On the Second instance you should see (Mirror, Synchronized/Restoring) next to Sales.

4. The label for the Sales database will show you what role it plays in the database-mirroring session.

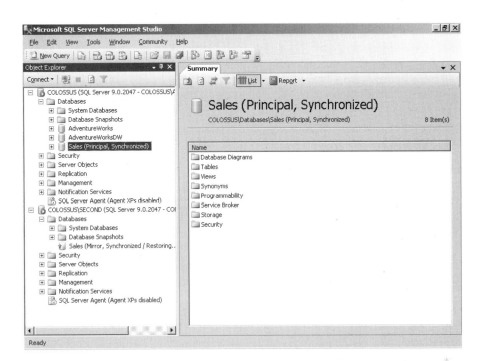

Exercise 20.2	Implementing Log Shipping
Scenario	Your accounting department has come to rely on SQL Server to get their work done. They need it to be up and running at all times during the day, so you know you need to implement some form of high availability. In the past, some contract workers, who were not familiar with your systems, accidentally updated the data incorrectly, and you do not want future mistakes to be propagated to the standby server right away. Bearing this in mind, you decide to implement log shipping so you can control the delay of the restore on the secondary server.
Duration	This task should take approximately 60 minutes.
Setup	For this task, you need access to the machine you installed SQL Server 2005 on in Exercise 2.1, the Second instance of SQL Server 2005 you installed in Exercise 2.2, and the AdventureWorks database installed with the sample data.
Caveat	This task doesn't have any caveats.
Procedure	In this task, you will make a backup of the AdventureWorks database and restore it to the Second instance of SQL Server in the RECOVERY state. You will then ship the AdventureWorks database logs to the Second instance.

Equipment Used	For this task, you need access to the machine you installed SQL Server 2005 on in Exercise 2.1, the Second instance of SQL Server 2005 you installed in Exercise 2.2, and the AdventureWorks database installed with the sample data.
Objective	To backup the AdventureWorks database from the default instance.
Criteria for Completion	This task is complete when you have successfully configured log shipping for the AdventureWorks database from the default instance on your machine to the Second instance.

■ PART A: Backing up AdventureWorks from the Default Instance

1. Open SQL Server Management Studio, expand Databases, right-click AdventureWorks, point to Tasks, and click Back Up.

2. In the Backup dialog box, make sure AdventureWorks is the selected database to back up and Backup Type is Full.

3. Leave the default name in the Name box. In the Description box, enter Full Backup of AdventureWorks.

4. Under Destination, a disk device may already be listed. If so, select the device, and click Remove.

5. Under Destination, click Add.

6. In the Select Backup Destination box, click File Name, and in the text box enter x:\temp\AdvWorks.bak (make sure the temp directory exists on the selected drive). Click OK.

7. Click OK to start the backup.

8. When the backup is complete, you will get a notification; click OK to close it.

■ PART B: Backing up the Transaction Log for AdventureWorks on the Default Instance

1. Open SQL Server Management Studio, expand Databases, right-click AdventureWorks, point to Tasks, and click Back Up.

2. In the Backup dialog box, make sure AdventureWorks is the selected database to back up and Backup Type is Transaction Log.

3. Leave the default name in the Name box. In the Description box, enter Transaction Log Backup of AdventureWorks.

4. Make sure x:\temp\AdventureWorks.bak (the same device used in Step 6 in the previous set of steps) is the only device listed.

5. Click OK to start the backup.

6. When the backup is complete, you will get a notification; click OK to close it.

■ PART C: Restoring the Database to the Second Instance

1. Open SQL Server Management Studio, and connect to the Second instance by selecting Server\SECOND from the Server Name drop-down list.

2. Right-click Databases, and select Restore Database.

3. Enter AdventureWorks in the To Database box.

4. Under Source for Restore, select From Device. Click the ellipsis (…) button next to the text box to select a device.

5. In the Specify Backup dialog box, select File from the Backup Media drop-down list box, and click Add.

6. In the Locate Backup File dialog box, find the AdventureWorks.bak file, and click OK.

7. Click OK to close the Specify Backup dialog box.

8. Under Select the Backup Sets to Restore, check the boxes for both backups of AdventureWorks.

9. On the Options page, in the Restore the Database Files As grid, under the Restore As column, make these changes so you do not accidentally overwrite the original AdventureWorks data and log files:

   - Change AdventureWorks_data.mdf to AdventureWorks_data_ls.mdf.
   - Change AdventureWorks_log.ldf to AdventureWorks_log_ls.ldf.
   - Change AdventureWorks Catalog to AdventureWorks Catalog LS (if it exists).

10. Also on the Options page, make sure the RESTORE WITH STANDBY option is selected.

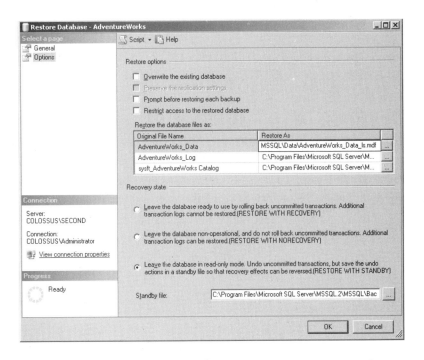

11. Click OK to begin the restore process.

12. Click OK in the dialog box that opens after the restore is complete.

■ PART D: Configuring Log Shipping

1. Open SQL Server Management Studio, and connect to the default instance.

2. Expand Databases, right-click AdventureWorks, point to Tasks, and click Ship Transaction Logs.

3. Check the box next to Enable This As a Primary Database in a Log Shipping Configuration.

4. Click the Backup Settings button.

5. Enter a network path for the backup folder by typing \\<YourServerName>\c$\temp in the first text box.

6. Enter a local path for the backup folder by typing x:\temp in the second text box.

7. Select the defaults for the job schedules and file deletion, and click OK to return to the Database Properties dialog box.

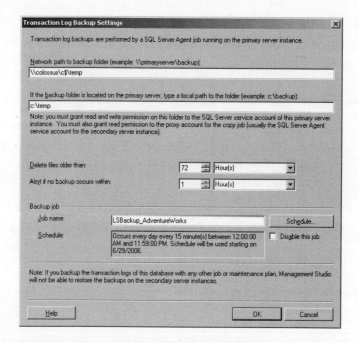

8. Click the Add button under the Secondary Server Instances and Databases grid.

9. Click the Connect button next to the Secondary Server Instance text box, and connect to the Second instance.

10. On the Initialize Secondary Database tab, make sure the No, the Secondary Database Is Initialized option is selected.

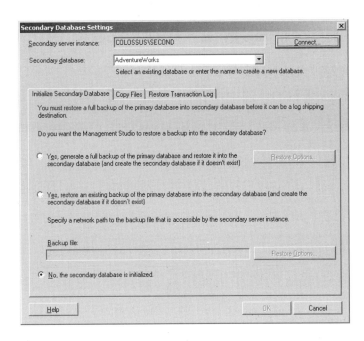

11. On the Copy Files tab, enter x:\temp\copy (make sure this subdirectory exists in temp).

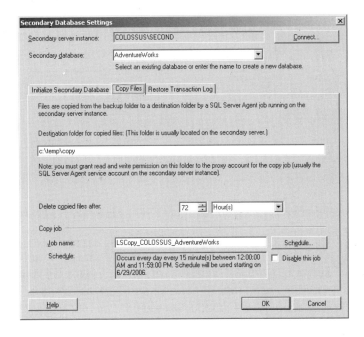

12. On the Restore Transaction Log tab, select the Standby Mode option to allow users read-only access to the standby database.

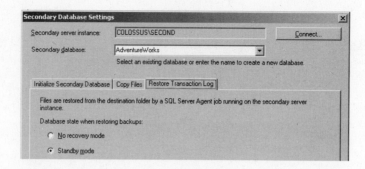

13. Click OK to return to the Database Properties dialog box.

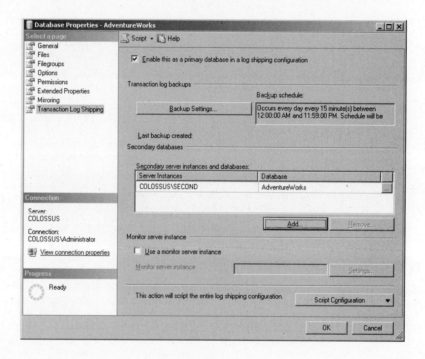

14. Click OK again to finish configuring log shipping.
15. Close the Configuration dialog box when it is complete.

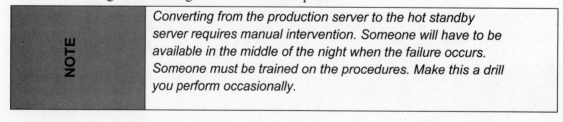

> **NOTE**
>
> *Converting from the production server to the hot standby server requires manual intervention. Someone will have to be available in the middle of the night when the failure occurs. Someone must be trained on the procedures. Make this a drill you perform occasionally.*

■ PART E: Verifying Results

You can tell whether you are successful by following these steps:

1. Open a new query in SQL Server Management Studio.
2. From the Query menu, hover over Connection, and click Change Connection.

3. Connect to the default instance of SQL Server.

4. To create a new record to ship to the Second instance, enter and execute the following code:

```
USE AdventureWorks

GO

INSERT  HumanResources.Shift(Name,  StartTime,  EndTime,  ModifiedDate)
VALUES('Test Shift 3', getdate() + 1, getdate()+ 2, getdate())
```

5. Wait approximately 15 minutes for the log-shipping jobs to run.

6. Clear the query window. From the Query menu, hover over Connection, and click Change Connection.

7. Connect to the Second instance of SQL Server.

8. Run this query to see whether the log was successfully shipped:

```
USE AdventureWorks SELECT * FROM HumanResources.Shift
```

9. You should see the new Test Shift 3 record after the logs are shipped. If the logs do not ship, make sure the SQL Server Agent is running on both instances.

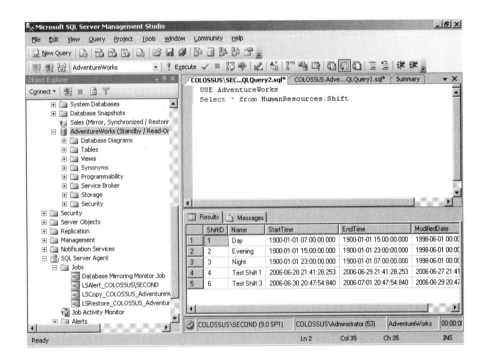

Exercise 20.3	Creating a Database Snapshot
Scenario	You have created a new database for your engineering department to store their data, some of which is important test results for new products. Your chief engineer is naturally concerned about keeping the database available, but he does not want the database copied to another server for security reasons. You decide that the best way to protect against disaster, and get the data back as fast as possible, is to create a database snapshot.
Duration	This task should take approximately 30 minutes.

Setup	For this task, you need access to the machine you installed SQL Server 2005 on in Exercise 2.1.
Caveat	In production, you should give the snapshot a more descriptive name, using the date and time of the snapshot, because you can create more than one per day. A good example is Test_ Snapshot_20060629_1130AM.mdf. I'm using a short name to keep the task simple.
Procedure	In this task, you will create a new database named Test, create a new table in the database, and then create a snapshot of the new database.
Equipment Used	For this task, you need access to the machine you installed SQL Server 2005 on in Exercise 2.1.
Objective	To create a database snapshot.
Criteria for Completion	This task is complete when you have created a new database named Test, created a new table named TestResults in that database, and created a snapshot of the new Test database.

■ PART A: Creating the Test Database and Inserting a New Table

1. Start SQL Server Management Studio by selecting Start, Programs, Microsoft SQL Server 2005, and Management Studio.

2. Connect to your default instance of SQL Server.

3. Right-click Databases, and choose New Database from the context menu.

4. On the General page of the Database properties sheet, enter the database name Test, and leave the owner as <default>.

5. Accept the all the defaults, and click OK to create the Test database.

6. In Object Explorer, expand the Test database.

7. Right-click the Tables icon, and select New Table to open the table designer.

8. In the first row, under Column Name, enter ProdID with a datatype of int, and uncheck Allow Nulls.

9. In the second row under Column Name, enter Results with a datatype of nvarchar(100), and uncheck Allow Nulls.

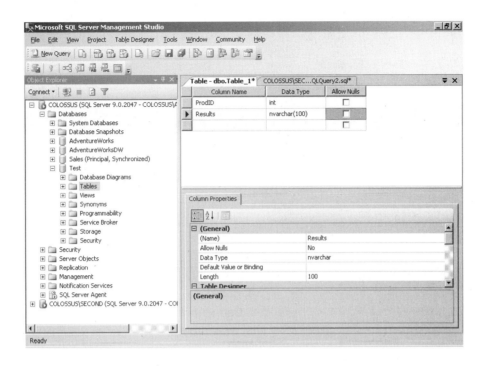

10. Click the Save button (it looks like a floppy disk) on the left side of the toolbar.

11. In the Choose Name box that opens, enter TestResults.

12. Close the table designer screen by clicking the X in the upper-right corner of the window.

13. To create a new record in the TestResults table, enter and execute the following code:

```
USE Test INSERT dbo.TestResults(ProdID,Results) VALUES(1,'Success')
```

■ PART B: Creating a Snapshot of the Test Database

1. Open a new query in SQL Server Management Studio.

2. To create a snapshot of Test on the C drive, execute the following code (note that you should replace the C:\ with the drive on which you installed SQL Server):

```
CREATE DATABASE Test_Snapshot ON ( NAME = Test, FILENAME =
'c:\Program Files\Microsoft SQL Server\MSSQL.1\MSSQL\data\
Test_snapshot.mdf' ) AS SNAPSHOT OF Test
```

3. In the results pane (on the bottom) in the query window, you should see a message stating that the command completed successfully.

4. To verify that the snapshot has been created, expand your server in Object Explorer, and then expand Database Snapshots. You should see Test_Snapshot in the list of available snapshots.

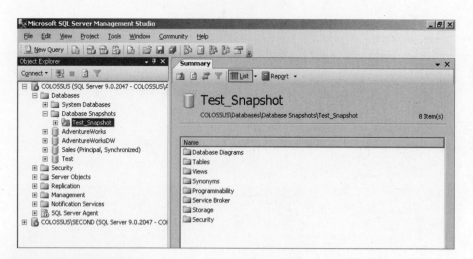

Question 2	Your management decrees that no more than ten minutes of data shall be lost under any circumstances. Can you create a snapshot every ten minutes? If yes, what are the costs? What are the procedures? What are the alternative methods? Log shipping every ten minutes? Log backup every ten minutes?

■ PART C: Verifying Results

1. Open a new query in SQL Server Management Studio.
2. To create a new record in the TestResults table, enter and execute the following code:

```
USE Test INSERT dbo.TestResults(ProdID,Results) VALUES(2,'Fail')
```

3. Clear the query window, and run this query to see whether the update was applied to the snapshot:

```
USE Test_snapshot SELECT * FROM dbo.TestResults
```

4. You should see only the record that existed before that snapshot was taken, which is the ProdID: 1, Results: Success record.

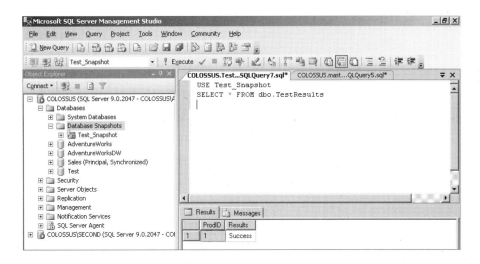

Exercise 20.4	Reverting from a Database Snapshot
Scenario	Your chief engineer recently asked you to help protect his database and keep it available, so you decided to create regular snapshots of the database. Today, one of the engineers accidentally updated several records in the database, indicating that several products had passed safety tests when in fact they had failed, and the engineer doesn't remember which records were updated in error. You need to get the database back to the point before the errors were introduced, so you decide that the fastest method is to revert from the most recent snapshot.
Duration	This task should take approximately 15 minutes.
Setup	For this task, you need access to the machine you installed SQL Server 2005 on in Exercise 2.1 and the Test database and Test_Snapshot database snapshot you created in Exercise 20.3.
Caveat	In a production environment, you should perform a full backup of your database after reverting from a snapshot.
Procedure	In this task, you will revert the Test database from the Test_Snapshot database snapshot.
Equipment Used	For this task, you need access to the machine you installed SQL Server 2005 on in Exercise 2.1 and the Test database and the Test_Snapshot database snapshot you created in Exercise 20.3.
Objective	To revert from a database snapshot.
Criteria for Completion	This task is complete when you have reverted from the Test_Snapshot database snapshot.

■ PART A: Creating the Test Database and Inserting a New Table

1. Start SQL Server Management Studio by selecting Start Programs, Microsoft SQL Server 2005 and Management Studio.

2. To view all the records in the TestResults table of the original database, run the following query (you should see two records):

```
USE Test SELECT * FROM TestResults
```

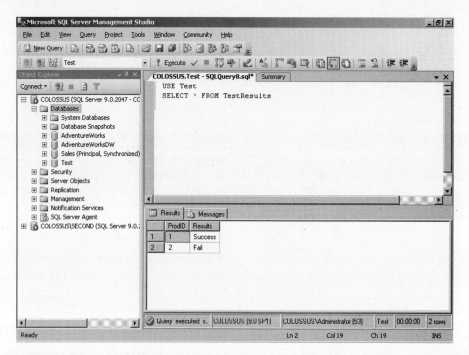

3. To view all the records in the TestResults table of the snapshot, run the following query (you should see one record):

```
USE Test_Snapshot SELECT * FROM TestResults
```

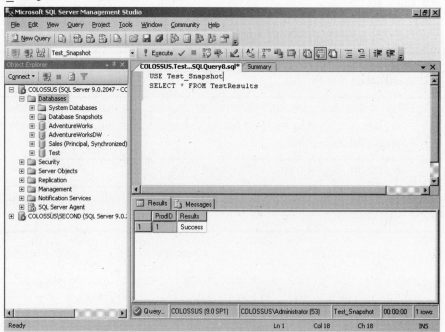

4. To revert from the snapshot, clear the query window, and enter and execute the following code:

```
USE Master RESTORE DATABASE Test FROM DATABASE_SNAPSHOT = 'Test_Snapshot'
```

5. Your original database should now match your snapshot. To view all the records in the TestResults table of the original database, run the following query (you should now see one record):

```
USE Test SELECT * FROM TestResults
```

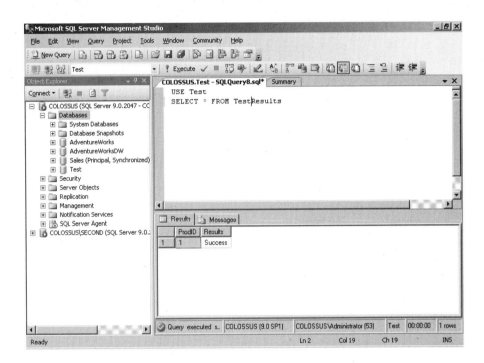

6. To remove the now defunct snapshot, expand Database Snapshots in Object Explorer, right-click Test_Snapshot, and click Delete.

7. Click OK in the Delete an Object dialog box.

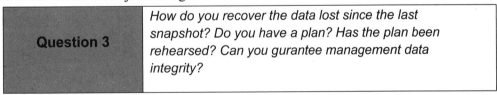

Question 3	How do you recover the data lost since the last snapshot? Do you have a plan? Has the plan been rehearsed? Can you gurantee management data integrity?

■ PART B: Verifying Results

1. Examine the data in the original TestResults table of the Test database.
2. You will have only one surviving record.

LAB 21
WORKING WITH SERVICE BROKER

This lab contains the following exercise and activity:

Exercise 21.1   Creating a Service Broker Object

Exercise 21.1	Creating a Service Broker Object
Scenario	The Marketing Department at your company wants to send a welcome e-mail message to new customers who register on the company's Web site. To minimize the impact to the site's scalability, the senior database developer has decided to implement this functionality through a service that will be invoked asynchronously when a new user registers.
Duration	This task should take approximately 60 minutes.
Setup	For this task, you need access to the machine you installed SQL Server 2005 on in Exercise 2.1 and the Sales database you created in Exercise 5.1.
Caveat	There are no caveats for this exercise.
Procedure	In this task, you will create the objects needed for a service broker instance and test it.
Equipment Used	For this task, you need access to the machine you installed SQL Server 2005 on in Exercise 2.1 and the Sales database you created in Exercise 5.1.
Objective	To send an e-mail asynchronously.
Criteria for Completion	This task is complete when you verify the e-mail's creation.

■ PART A: Performing the Following Procedure to Create Service Broker Objects

1. Click Start, point to All Programs, point to Microsoft SQL Server 2005, and then click SQL Server Management Studio.
2. In the Connect to Server dialog box, specify the values in the following table, and then click Connect:

Property	Value
Server type	Database Engine
Server name	<YourComputerName>
Authentication	Windows Authentication

3. Start a new query editor session.

■ PART B: Enabling Service Broker in the Sales Database

1. Review the following code. Enter it into the Query Editor:

```
USE master;
GO


-- Enable Service Broker in the Sales database
ALTER DATABASE Sales SET ENABLE_BROKER;
```

2. Execute the code.

■ PART C: Creating a Master Key in the Sales Database

1. Review the following code. Enter it into the Query Editor:

```
-- Configure the Sales database
USE Sales
GO


IF   NOT   EXISTS   (SELECT   *   FROM   sys.symmetric_keys   WHERE   name   =
'##MS_DatabaseMasterKey##')
CREATE MASTER KEY ENCRYPTION BY PASSWORD = 'Pa$$w0rd';
GO
```

2. Execute the code.

■ PART D: Creating a New Schema Named EMail in the AdventureWorks Database

1. Review the following code. Enter it into your Query Editor:

```
    CREATE SCHEMA EMail
    GO
```

2. Execute the code.

■ PART E: Creating a New Table Named EMail.EmailLog in the AdventureWorks Database

1. Review the following code. Enter it into your Query Editor:

```
-- Create a table to log details of the customer emails sent
CREATE TABLE EMail.EmailLog
(  Date datetime NOT NULL,
    [Event] nvarchar(50) NOT NULL,
    CustomerData xml)
GO
```

2. Execute the code.

■ PART F: Creating Service Broker Objects

1. Review the following code. Enter it into your Query Editor:

```
USE Sales
GO


-- Create message types that will be used to pass customer
-- data to the EmailService service
CREATE MESSAGE TYPE [//Training.com/EMail/CustomerDetails]
VALIDATION = WELL_FORMED_XML
GO


-- Create a contract that will be supported by the
-- EmailService service
CREATE CONTRACT [//Training.com/EMail/SendCustomerDetails]
(  [//Training.com/EMail/CustomerDetails]
    SENT BY INITIATOR)
GO


-- Create two queues that will be used by the EMailService service
CREATE QUEUE Email.NewCustomerQueue
WITH STATUS = ON

CREATE QUEUE EMail.NewCustomerEmailQueue
WITH STATUS = OFF
GO


-- Create a service which calls the EmailService to send
-- an e-mail message to a new customer
CREATE SERVICE [//Training.com/Email/CustomerService]
ON QUEUE Email.NewCustomerQueue

-- Create the EmailService service which sends an e-mail
-- message to a new customer
```

```
CREATE SERVICE [//Training.com/EMail/EmailService]
ON QUEUE EMail.NewCustomerEmailQueue
([//Training.com/EMail/SendCustomerDetails])
```

2. Click the Execute button on the toolbar to execute the query.

3. In Object Explorer, expand Databases, Sales, and Service Broker, Expand Message Types, Contracts, Queues, and Services, and then show the various objects that you just created.

■ PART G: Preparing to Send and Receive Messages

1. Review the following code. Enter it into your Query Editor:

```
USE Sales
GO

-- Sends messages from the CustomerService service to the
-- EmailService service
CREATE PROCEDURE Email.uspEmailNewCustomer
    @firstName nvarchar(50),
    @lastName nvarchar(50),
    @emailAddress nvarchar(50)
AS
BEGIN
SET NOCOUNT ON;

-- Create message body to pass to SendMail service.
DECLARE @message xml

SET @message = NCHAR(0xFEFF)
+ '<Customer>'
+ '<CustomerName>' + @firstName + ' ' + @lastName + '</CustomerName>'
+ '<EmailAddress>' + @emailAddress + '</EmailAddress>'
+ '</Customer>'

DECLARE @dialogHandle UNIQUEIDENTIFIER

BEGIN DIALOG @dialogHandle
FROM SERVICE [//Training.com/Sales/CustomerService]
TO SERVICE '//Training.com/EMail/EmailService'
ON CONTRACT [//Training.com/EMail/SendCustomerDetails];

SEND ON CONVERSATION @dialogHandle
MESSAGE TYPE [//Training.com/EMail/CustomerDetails] (@message)

    END CONVERSATION @dialogHandle
END;
GO
```

```
--Processes messages received by the EmailService service
CREATE PROCEDURE EMail.uspSendCustomerEmail
AS
BEGIN
SET NOCOUNT ON;

DECLARE @conversation UNIQUEIDENTIFIER
DECLARE @msg NVARCHAR(MAX)
DECLARE @msgType NVARCHAR(256)

;RECEIVE TOP(1)
    @conversation = conversation_handle,
    @msgType = message_type_name,
    @msg = message_body
FROM Sales.EMail.NewCustomerEmailQueue

IF (@@ROWCOUNT = 0) RETURN

IF (@msgType = '//Training.com/EMail/CustomerDetails')
    BEGIN
-- Extract data from the message
    DECLARE @emailAddress nvarchar(30)
    DECLARE @hDoc int
    EXECUTE sp_xml_preparedocument @hdoc OUTPUT, @msg
    SELECT @emailAddress = EmailAddress
    FROM OPENXML(@hDoc, 'Customer', 2)
    WITH
    (EmailAddress nvarchar(30))
    EXECUTE sp_xml_removedocument @hDoc

-- Code to send the email would go here

-- Log the email
    INSERT INTO Sales.EMail.EmailLog
    (Date, [Event], CustomerData)
    VALUES
    (getdate(), 'Email sent to ' + @emailAddress, @msg);
END

ELSE IF (@msgType =
'http://schemas.microsoft.com/SQL/ServiceBroker/Error') OR
(@msgType = 'http://schemas.microsoft.com/SQL/ServiceBroker/EndDialog')

END CONVERSATION @conversation

ELSE
    BEGIN
    END CONVERSATION @conversation
    WITH ERROR = 500 DESCRIPTION = 'Invalid message type.';
```

```
     INSERT INTO Sales.EMail.EmailLog (Date, [Event], CustomerData)
     VALUES (getdate(), 'Invalid message type', @msg);
     END
END;
GO


ALTER QUEUE EMail.NewCustomerEmailQueue
WITH STATUS = ON,
ACTIVATION (
    STATUS = ON,
    PROCEDURE_NAME = Sales.EMail.uspSendCustomerEmail,
    MAX_QUEUE_READERS = 5,
    EXECUTE AS SELF)
```

2. Click the Execute button on the toolbar to execute the query.

■ PART H: Sending a message

1. Select and execute the following EXECUTE statement to send a message to the EmailService service:

```
EXECUTE Sales.Email.uspEmailNewCustomer
        @firstName = 'Alice',
        @lastName = 'Jones',
        @emailAddress = 'Student@Training.com'
```

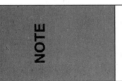 NOTE	*In your real world, you would need to configure your mailboxes (POP3 server) to acknowledge Student and the Training domain.*

■ PART I: Verifying Results

1. Select and execute the following SELECT statement to show that the EmailService service has processed the message:

```
SELECT * FROM Sales.EMail.EmailLog
```

LAB 22
WORKING WITH ENDPOINTS

This lab contains the following exercise and activity:

Exercise 22.1   Working with Endpoints

Exercise 22.1	Working with Endpoints
Scenario	Your boss asked you to review endpoints. You checked Books Online and discovered there are four types: SOAP, TSQL, SERVICE_BROKER, and DATABASE_MIRRORING. You want to learn the syntax differences between them.
Duration	This task should take approximately 15 minutes.
Setup	For this task, you need access to the machine you installed SQL Server 2005 on in Exercise 2.1 and Books Online.
Caveat	There are no caveats for this exercise.
Procedure	Review the syntax differences between the four endpoint types using examples you find in Books Online and the snippets in this exercise.
Equipment Used	For this task, you need access to the machine you installed SQL Server 2005 on in Exercise 2.1 and Books Online.
Objective	To understand endpoints.
Criteria for Completion	This task is complete when you have understood the requirements, purpose, and permissions for endpoints.

> **NOTE**
>
> *Currently there are no TSQL <language_specific_arguments>.*

■ PART A: Creating Endpoints for Service Broker

1. Review the following code for syntax requirements but do not execute:

```
USE Master
GO
CREATE ENDPOINT BrokerEndpoint
STATE = STARTED
AS TCP ( LISTENER_PORT = 4037 )
FOR SERVICE_BROKER ( AUTHENTICATION = WINDOWS ) ;
GO
```

■ PART B: Creating Endpoints for Database Mirroring

1. Review the following code for syntax requirements but do not execute:

```
-- Endpoint for intital principal server instance which is the only server
instance running on the first host.
CREATE ENDPOINT EndPointMirroring

STATE = STARTED

AS TCP (LISTENER_PORT = 7022)

FOR DATABASE_MIRRORING (ROLE = PARTNER)

GO

-- Endpoint for intital principal server instance which is the only server
instance running on the second host.
CREATE ENDPOINT EndPointMirroring

STATE = STARTED

AS TCP (LISTENER_PORT = 7022)

FOR DATABASE_MIRRORING (ROLE = PARTNER)

GO

-- Endpoint for intital principal server instance which is the only server
instance running on the third host.
CREATE ENDPOINT EndPointMirroring

STATE = STARTED

AS TCP (LISTENER_PORT = 7022)

FOR DATABASE_MIRRORING (ROLE = WITNESS)

GO
```

■ PART C: Creating HTTP Endpoints

1. Review the following code for syntax requirements but do not execute:

```
USE Sales

GO
```

```
CREATE ENDPOINT Sql_Endpoint
STATE = STARTED
AS HTTP (
    PATH = '/SQL',
    AUTHENTICATION = (INTEGRATED),
    PORTS = (CLEAR),
    SITE = '<YourServerName>')
FOR SOAP (
    WEBMETHOD 'GetSqlInfo'
    -- Note that 'GetSqlInfo is an existing stored procedure or user
    -- defined function. The WEBMETHOD line can be repeated for as
    -- many procedures or functions you wish to expose.
    (name = 'master.dbo.sp_msver',
    ( SCHEMA = STANDARD ),
    -- You may also specify the schema as a parameter with the name,
    -- like this: "( name = 'AdventureWorks.dbo.ProductList',
    -- SCHEMA = STANDARD ),
    WEBMETHOD 'DayAsNumber'
    (name = 'master.sys.fn_MSDayAsNumber' ),
    WSDL = DEFAULT,
    SCHEMA = STANDARD.
    DATABASE = 'master'
    NAMESPACE = 'http://Training.Com/');
GO
```

■ PART D: Creating Endpoints for Network Protocols

1. Look up "Network Protocols, and TDS Endpoints" in Books Online. Examine the definition of an endpoint for a tabular data stream. Note especially that additional endpoints can be created.

■ PART E: Managing Permissions on Endpoints

1. Review the following code for syntax requirements but do not execute:

```
USE Master
GO
GRANT CONNECT ON ENDPOINT::Sql_Endpoint to RSmith;
-- Other permissions include: ALTER, CONTROL, TAKE OWNERSHIP, and
-- VIEW DEFINITION
GO
```

LAB 23
WORKING WITH REPLICATION

This lab contains the following exercises and activities:

Exercise 23.1	Choosing a Replication Type
Scenario	You work for a medium-sized company that has offices throughout the world. Many of the users in these offices need access to the data stored on SQL Server, and they need it as fast as possible. You know that the best way to get this data to the users is via replication; however, before you can configure replication, you need to figure out which type of replication to use.

Duration	This task should take approximately 15 minutes.
Setup	You don't need to perform any setup for this task because it is all takes place on paper.
Caveat	This task doesn't have any caveats.
Procedure	In this task, you will read each scenario and decide on the proper replication type.
Equipment Used	The only equipment you need for this task is some paper and a pencil or pen.
Objective	To choose the correct replication type.
Criteria for Completion	This task is complete when you have chosen the correct replication type for each of the scenarios presented.

■ PART A: Choosing the Best Solution

NOTE

Replication is yet another way to create redundant data in case disaster destroys one's data center. Replication is also a method to reduce wide-area networking costs in a distributed environment. Replication is overhead-expensive. Do you have machines able to handle both the production needs and the replication needs? Consider both the dollar costs and user response time in choosing first whether you will use replication and second whether it represents the best solution.

1. One of your servers, located in New York City, contains a Sales database that needs to be replicated to your satellite offices in Berlin, London, and Moscow, which are connected via a partial T1 connection that consistently runs at 80 percent capacity. Your sales associates make changes to the database regularly throughout the day, but the users in the satellite offices do not need to see the changes immediately. Which type of replication should you use?

   a. Merge

   b. Transactional

   c. Snapshot

   d. Transactional with updating subscribers

   e. Snapshot with updating subscribers

2. Each branch office of your company has its own accounting department. The network connections between the branch offices are reliable, but they are consistently at 80 percent usage during the day. Each of your branch office accounting departments needs a copy of the main accounting database that they can update locally, and they need it to be as current as possible. Which replication type best suits your needs?

   a. Merge

   b. Transactional

   c. Snapshot

    d. Transactional with immediate updating subscribers

    e. Snapshot with updating subscribers

3. Several of your company's sales offices are located throughout the country. Headquarters needs an up-to-date copy of the sales offices' databases. When headquarters sends new inventory to the sales offices, they want to update the database at headquarters and have the new data replicated to the respective sales offices. Which replication type should you use?

    a. Merge

    b. Transactional

    c. Snapshot

    d. Transactional with immediate updating subscribers

    e. Snapshot with updating subscribers

4. The retail division of your company manages shops in various cities. Each shop maintains its own inventory database. The retail manager in Phoenix wants each of her four shops to be able to share inventory with each other so employees can pick up a part from another nearby store rather than waiting for a shipment from the manufacturer. To do this, employees at each shop should be able to update their local copy of the inventory database, decrement the other store's inventory, and then go pick up the part. This way, the other store won't sell its part because the part will have already been taken out of stock. Which replication type should you use to accomplish this?

    a. Merge

    b. Transactional

    c. Snapshot

    d. Transactional with updating subscribers

    e. Snapshot with updating subscribers

■ PART B: Verifying Results

1. **Scenario 1:** The answer is b. Because the entire database does not change every day, you do not need to use the snapshot type. Also, the snapshot type would use a great deal more bandwidth than the transactional type. Because the subscribers do not need to update their copy of the data, you do not need the added complexity of merging or updating subscribers. Also, you do not have much network bandwidth to play with, and transactional replication uses the least amount of bandwidth.

2. **Scenario 2:** The answer is d. Because the network is running close to capacity most of the time, it would not support snapshot replication. Because the users would be updating only their own data, merge replication would be overkill. Transactional with updating subscribers fits your needs because the network usage is lower than snapshot and still allows users to update local copies of the data.

3. **Scenario 3:** The answer is d. Because each office needs to be able to update their own inventory databases each time they make a sale and headquarters needs to be able to update the main database, you need to give the sales offices the capability to update. Merge replication would be overkill here because each sales office does not need to update other sales offices' data.

4. **Scenario 4:** The answer is a. In this scenario, you do not have a central "main" database that each subscriber will update. All the stores must be able to update data for the other stores' data. The best way to accomplish this is through merge replication.

Exercise 23.2	Designing a Replication Topology
Scenario	You work for a medium-sized company that has offices throughout the world. Many of the users in these offices need access to the data stored on SQL Server, and they need it as fast as possible. You know that the best way to get this data to the users is via replication; however, before you can configure replication, you need to decide on a replication topology.
Duration	This task should take approximately 15 minutes.
Setup	You don't need to perform any setup for this task because it is all takes place on paper.
Caveat	This task doesn't have any caveats.
Procedure	In this task, you will read each scenario and decide on the proper replication topology.
Equipment Used	The only equipment you need for this task is some paper and a pencil or pen.
Objective	To choose the correct replication topology.
Criteria for Completion	This task is complete when you have chosen the correct replication type for each of the scenarios presented.

■ PART A: Choosing the Correct Replication Topology

1. One of your servers, located in New York City, contains a Sales database that needs to be replicated to your satellite offices in Berlin, London, and Moscow, which are connected via a partial T1 connection that consistently runs at 80 percent capacity. Your sales associates make changes to the database regularly throughout the day, but the users in the satellite offices do not need to see the changes immediately. You have decided to use transactional replication. Which replication topology should you use?

    a. Central subscriber/multiple publishers

    b. Multiple publishers/multiple subscribers

    c. Central publisher/central distributor

    d. Remote distribution

2. Each branch office of your company has its own accounting department. The network connections between the branch offices are reliable, but they are consistently at 80 percent usage during the day. Each of your branch office accounting departments needs a copy of the main accounting database that they can update locally, and they need it to be as current as possible. You have decided to use transactional replication with immediate updating subscribers. Which replication topology best suits your needs?

    a. Central subscriber/multiple publishers

    b. Multiple publishers/multiple subscribers

    c. Central publisher/central distributor

    d. Remote distribution

3. Several of your company's sales offices are located throughout the country. Headquarters needs an up-to-date copy of the sales offices' databases. When headquarters sends new inventory to the sales offices, they want to update the database at headquarters and have the new data replicated to the respective sales offices. You have decided to use transactional replication with immediate updating subscribers. Which replication topology should you use?

    a. Central subscriber/multiple publishers

    b. Multiple publishers/multiple subscribers

    c. Central publisher/central distributor

    d. Remote distribution

4. The retail division of your company manages shops in various cities. Each shop maintains its own inventory database. The retail manager in Phoenix wants each of her four shops to be able to share inventory with each other so employees can pick up a part from another nearby store rather than waiting for a shipment from the manufacturer. To do this, employees at each shop should be able to update their local copy of the inventory database, decrement the other store's inventory, and then go pick up the part. This way, the other store won't sell its part because the part will have already been taken out of stock. You have decided to use merge replication. Which replication topology should you use?

    a. Central subscriber/multiple publishers

    b. Multiple publishers/multiple subscribers

    c. Central publisher/central distributor

    d. Remote distribution

■ PART B: Verifying Results

1. **Scenario 1:** The answer is d. The models that involve multiple publishers obviously won't work here because you have only one publisher. The remote distributor option can save long-distance charges because instead of making several long-distance calls from New York to the satellites, you can place a distributor in London and let the distributor make less-expensive calls to the remaining satellites.

2. **Scenario 2:** Either answer c or answer d is acceptable here. Because you are using transactional replication with updating subscribers, you can use a central publisher at headquarters with each sales office being a subscriber.

3. **Scenario 3:** As with scenario 2, either answer c or answer d is acceptable. Because you are using transactional replication with updating subscribers, you can use a central publisher at headquarters with each sales office being a subscriber.

4. **Scenario 4:** The answer is b. Each store will publish its inventory database and subscribe to the other stores' inventory databases. This makes it the perfect scenario for a multiple publishers/multiple subscribers model.

Exercise 23.3	Configuring Replication
Scenario	You work for a medium-sized company that has offices throughout the world. Many of the users in these offices need access to the data stored on SQL Server, and they need it as fast as possible. You know that the best way to get this data to the users is via replication; however, before you can create publications and subscriptions, you must configure a distribution server.
Duration	This task should take approximately 30 minutes.
Setup	For this task, you need access to the machine you installed SQL Server 2005 on in Exercise 2.1.
Caveat	Make sure the SQL Server Agent is set to start automatically before starting this task.
Procedure	In this task, you will configure the default instance of SQL Server on your machine as a distribution server.
Equipment Used	For this task, you need access to the machine you installed SQL Server 2005 on in Exercise 2.1.
Objective	To configure your default instance as a distribution server.
Criteria for Completion	This task is complete when you have configured your default instance of SQL Server to act as a distributor.

■ PART A: Configuring Replication

1. Open SQL Server Management Studio, and connect to your server.
2. Right-click Replication, and click Configure Distribution.
3. You are presented with a welcome screen; click Next to continue.
4. The Distributor screen appears. Select the server that will act as its own distributor option, and click Next.

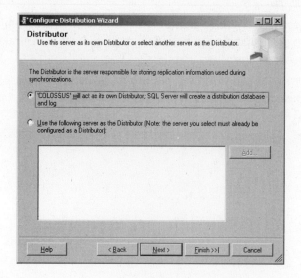

5. If your SQL Server agent is not configured to start automatically, you may be presented with a screen asking you to configure the agent. Set it to start automatically, and click Next.

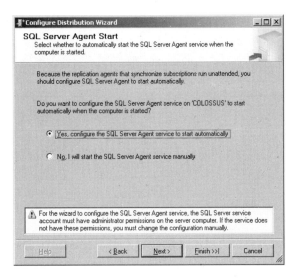

6. You are now asked to specify the snapshot folder. A good reason to change this is if you are replicating over the Internet and need to specify a folder that is accessible via FTP. Accept the defaults, and click Next.

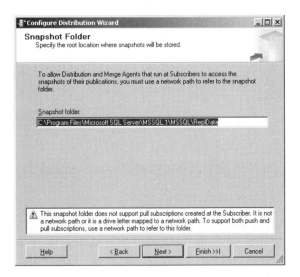

7. The Distribution Database screen appears next. You can supply a name for the distribution database as well as location information for its database file and transaction log. Keep the defaults, and click Next to continue.

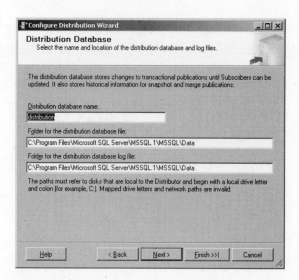

8. Now you are on the Publishers screen where you can choose which servers you want to configure as publishers. Clicking the ellipsis (…) button allows you to specify security credentials such as login ID and password, as well as the location of the snapshot folder. Be sure to place a check mark next to your local SQL Server system, and then click Next to continue.

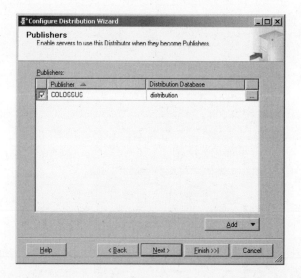

9. On the Wizard Actions screen, you can have the wizard configure distribution, write a script to configure distribution that you can run later, or do both. Leave the Configure Distribution box checked, and click Next to continue.

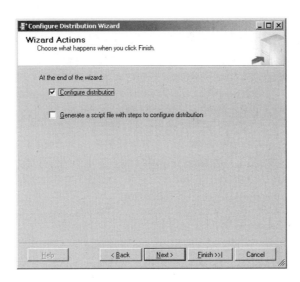

10. On the Complete the Wizard screen, review your selections, and click Finish.

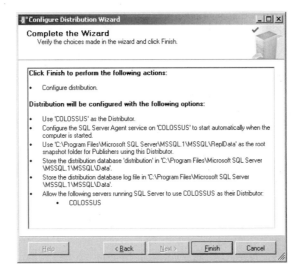

11. When the wizard is finished, click Close.

Question 1	The distributor can be anywhere; it does not need to be cohosted with the publisher. Also note the default folder for the distributor. What is it?

■ PART B: Verifying Results

1. Right-click Replication in Object Explorer; you should see an option labeled Distributor Properties. When you click that option, you should see dialog box confirming successful results.

Exercise 23.4	Creating a Transactional Publication
Scenario	You work for a medium-sized company that has offices throughout the world. The sales department in the Fresno branch office needs access to some of the data stored in the main database housed on the SQL Server at the corporate headquarters. They do not need the data immediately, so there is room for some latency; in addition, they are connected by a partial T1 that is at about 80 percent capacity, so there is little room for more traffic. Bearing these factors in mind, you decide the best way to get the data to the users in Fresno is to configure a transactional publication.
Duration	This task should take approximately 30 minutes.
Setup	For this task, you need access to the machine you installed SQL Server 2005 on in Exercise 2.1, the AdventureWorks database installed with the sample data, and the default instance of SQL Server you configured as a distributor in Exercise 23.3.
Caveat	If you still have log shipping enabled on the AdventureWorks database (from Exercise 20.2), you will need to disable it. Here's how: 1. Open SQL Server Management Studio, and connect to the default instance. 2. Expand Databases, right-click AdventureWorks, point to Tasks, and click Ship Transaction Logs. 3. Uncheck the box next to Enable This as a Primary Database in a Log Shipping Configuration. 4. Click Yes on the subsequent dialog box, and then click OK. 5. Click Close when the configuration is complete.
Procedure	In this task, you will create a transactional publication on your default instance of SQL Server on the Production.ProductCategory table in the AdventureWorks database.
Equipment Used	For this task, you need access to the machine you installed SQL Server 2005 on in Exercise 2.1, the AdventureWorks database installed with the sample data, and the default instance of SQL Server you configured as a distributor in Exercise 23.3.
Objective	To create a transactional publication on the Production.ProductCategory table.
Criteria for Completion	This task is complete when you have created a transactional publication based on the Production.ProductCategory table in the AdventureWorks database on the default instance of SQL Server.

■ PART A: Creating a Transactional Publication

1. Open SQL Server Management Studio, and connect to your SQL Server.

2. Expand Replication, right-click Local Publications, and click New Publication. This brings you to the New Publication Wizard welcome screen.

3. Click Next to continue.

4. On the Publication Database screen, highlight AdventureWorks, and click Next to continue.

5. On the Publication Type screen, you can choose what type of publication to create. For this task, choose Transactional Publication, and click Next to continue.

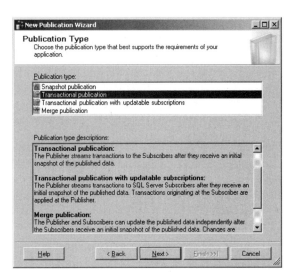

6. On the Articles screen, you can select what data and objects you want to replicate. Expand Tables, and check the ProductCategory box.

7. You can also set the properties for an article from this screen. Make sure ProductCategory is highlighted, click Article Properties, and then click Set Properties of Highlighted Table Article.

8. In the Destination Object section, change the destination object name to ReplicatedCategory, change the destination object owner to dbo, and click OK.

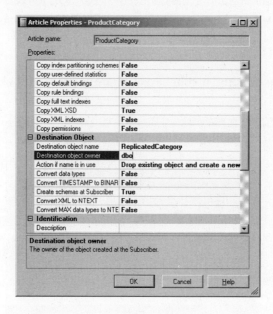

9. Back at the Articles screen, click Next to continue.

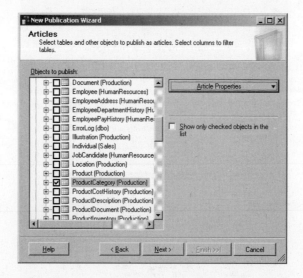

10. On the next screen, you can filter the data that is replicated. You do not want to filter the data in this case, so click Next to continue.

11. On the Snapshot Agent screen, check the box to create a snapshot immediately, and click Next.

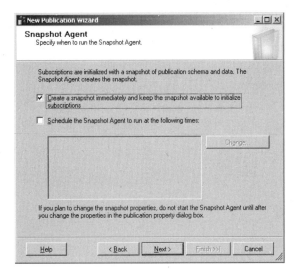

12. On the Agent Security screen, you are asked how the agents should log in and access data. To set this for the snapshot agent, click the Security Settings button next to Snapshot Agent.

13. Ordinarily you would create an account for the agent to run under, but to make the task simpler, you will run the agent using the SQL Server Agent account, so select the radio button for that option, and click OK.

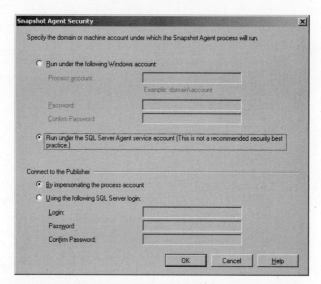

14. Back at the Agent Security screen, click Next to continue.

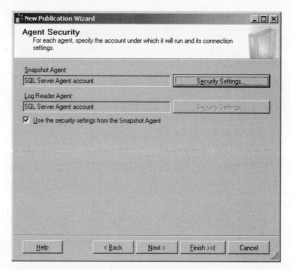

15. On the Wizard Actions screen, you can have the wizard create the publication, write a script to create the publication that you can run later, or do both. Leave the Create the Publication box checked, and click Next to continue.

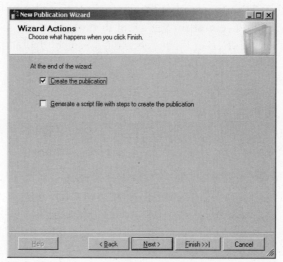

16. On the Complete the Wizard screen, you need to enter a name for the new publication, so enter CategoryPub, and click Finish.

17. When the wizard is finished, click Close.

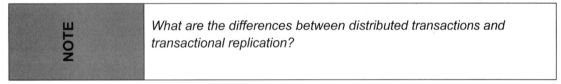

> **NOTE**
>
> *What are the differences between distributed transactions and transactional replication?*

■ PART B: Verifying Results

1. Open SQL Server Management Studio, connect to your SQL Server, and expand Replication. You should see the CategoryPub publication listed.

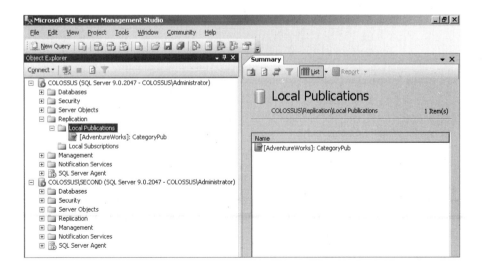

2. Right-click CategoryPub, and click Properties. The type should be Transactional.

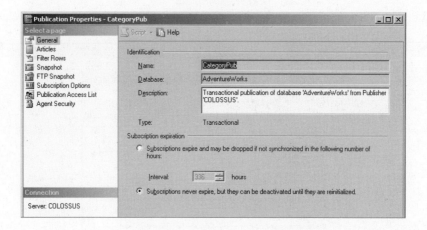

3. Click OK.

Exercise 23.5	Subscribing to a Transactional Publication
Scenario	You work for a medium-sized company that has offices throughout the world. The sales department in the Fresno branch office needs access to some of the data stored in the main database housed on the SQL Server at the corporate headquarters. They do not need the data immediately, so there is room for some latency; in addition, they are connected by a partial T1 that is at about 80 percent capacity, so there is little room for more traffic. You have already configured a transactional publication at headquarters; now you must create a subscription on the server in Fresno.
Duration	This task should take approximately 30 minutes.
Setup	For this task, you need access to the machine you installed SQL Server 2005 on in Exercise 2.1, the Second instance of SQL Server installed in Exercise 2.2, the AdventureWorks database installed with the sample data, the default instance of SQL Server configured as a distributor in Exercise 23.3, and the transactional publication configured in Exercise 23.4.
Caveat	Make sure the SQL Agent service for the Second instance is set to start automatically before starting this task.
Procedure	In this task, you will create a pull subscription to the transactional publication on your default instance of SQL Server.
Equipment Used	For this task, you need access to the machine you installed SQL Server 2005 on in Exercise 2.1, the Second instance of SQL Server installed in Exercise 2.2, the AdventureWorks database installed with the sample data, the default instance of SQL Server you configured as a distributor in Exercise 23.3, and the transactional publication you configured in Exercise 23.4.
Objective	To create a pull subscription to the transactional publication on the default instance of SQL Server.
Criteria for Completion	This task is complete when replication is running properly.

■ PART A: Subscribing to a Transactional Publication

1. Open SQL Server Management Studio, and connect to the Second instance by selecting it from the Server Name drop-down list.

2. Expand Replication, right-click Local Subscriptions, and click New Subscription. This brings you to the New Subscription Wizard welcome screen. Click Next to continue.

3. On the Publication screen, select the default instance of your server from the Publisher drop-down list (if it is not listed, select Find SQL Server Publisher), select CategoryPub from the Databases and Publications list, and click Next to continue.

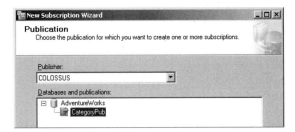

4. On the Distribution Agent Location screen, you are asked which machine should run the replication agents—at the distributor or at the subscriber. Because you want to create a pull subscription, select the Run Each Agent at Its Subscriber option, and click Next.

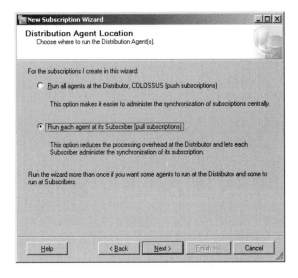

5. On the Subscribers screen, you can choose a subscriber for the publication. Check the box next to the Second instance of your server.

6. Then the drop-down list is populated with all the available databases on the subscriber. Select New Database from the list to open the New Database dialog box.

7. Enter TR_Test in the Database name box, and click OK. Then click Next.

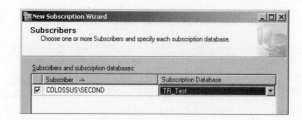

8. On the next screen you need to set the distribution agent security. To do so, click the ellipsis (...) button in the Subscription Properties list.

9. Ordinarily you would create an account for the agent to run under, but to make the task simpler, you will run the agent using the SQL Server Agent account, so select the radio button for that option, and click OK.

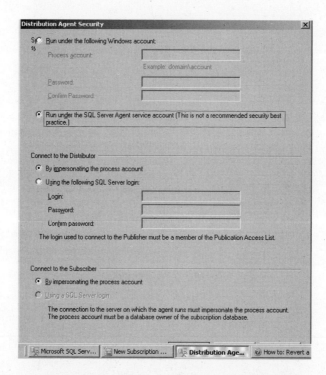

10. Back at the Distribution Agent Security screen, click Next to continue.

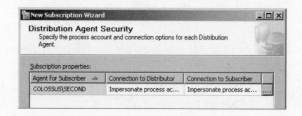

11. The next step is to set the synchronization schedule. Because you are using transactional replication, select Run Continuously, and click Next to continue.

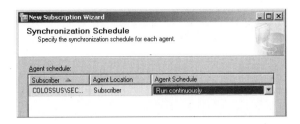

12. On the next screen, you can tell SQL Server when to initialize the subscription, if at all. If you have already created the schema on the subscriber, then you do not need to initialize the subscription. In this case, you should select Immediately from the drop-down list, make sure the Initialize box is checked, and click Next to continue.

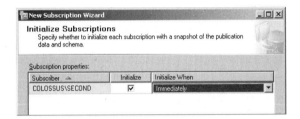

13. On the Wizard Actions screen, you can have the wizard create the subscription, write a script to create the subscription that you can run later, or do both. Leave the Create the Subscription box checked, and click Next to continue.

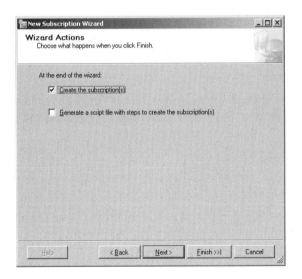

14. On the Complete the Wizard screen, review your options, and click Finish to create the subscription.

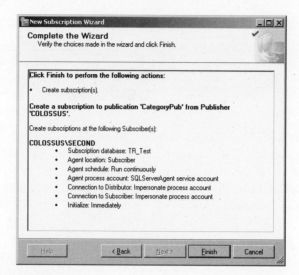

15. When the wizard is finished, click Close.

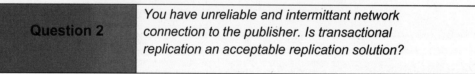

Question 2	You have unreliable and intermittant network connection to the publisher. Is transactional replication an acceptable replication solution?

■ PART B: Verifying Results

1. You should have four records in the ReplicatedCategory table. To verify that, open a new query, connect to the Second instance, and execute the following code:

```
USE TR_Test SELECT * FROM ReplicatedCategory
```

2. Now add a new record to the ProductCategory table in the AdventureWorks database on the default instance. Open a new query, and from the Query menu, select Connection and Change Connection. Then connect to the default instance.

3. Run the following code to add a new record:

```
USE AdventureWorks INSERT INTO Production.ProductCategory (Name)
VALUES ('Tools')
```

4. You should get the message that one row was added. Give the server about a minute to replicate the transaction, and then run the following query against the Second instance:

```
USE TR_Test SELECT * FROM ReplicatedCategory
```

5. You should get five records. The last record should be the new Tools record.

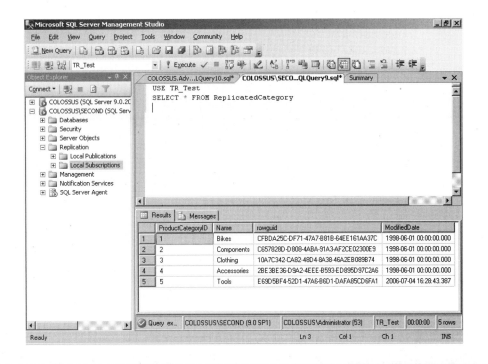

Exercise 23.6	Creating a Snapshot Publication
Scenario	You work for a medium-sized company that has offices throughout the world. The sales department in the Tucson branch office needs access to one of the databases housed on the SQL Server at the corporate headquarters. They will use the data only for reporting purposes, so they will not be making updates to their local copy of the data. They need the data to be refreshed only once a day, so you can allow for a full day of latency. They are connected by a partial T1 that is at about 75 percent capacity during peak hours, but off-hours it is at about 30 percent capacity, so the network has plenty of room during off-hours. Bearing these factors in mind, you decide that the best way to get the data to the users in Tucson is to configure a snapshot publication.
Duration	This task should take approximately 30 minutes.
Setup	For this task, you need access to the machine you installed SQL Server 2005 on in Exercise 2.1, the AdventureWorks database installed with the sample data, and the default instance of SQL Server you configured as a distributor in Exercise 23.3.
Caveat	If you still have log shipping enabled on the AdventureWorks database (from Exercise 20.2), you will need to disable it. Here's how: 1. Open SQL Server Management Studio, and connect to the default instance. 2. Expand Databases, right-click AdventureWorks, point to Tasks, and click Ship Transaction Logs. 3. Uncheck the box next to Enable This as a Primary Database in a Log Shipping configuration.

	4. Click Yes in the subsequent dialog box, and then click OK. 5. Click Close when the configuration is complete.
Procedure	In this task, you will create a snapshot publication on your default instance of SQL Server on the Person.AddressType table in the AdventureWorks database.
Equipment Used	For this task, you need access to the machine you installed SQL Server 2005 on in Exercise 2.1, the AdventureWorks database installed with the sample data, and the default instance of SQL Server you configured as a distributor in Exercise 23.3.
Objective	To create a snapshot publication.
Criteria for Completion	This task is complete when you have created a snapshot publication based on the Person.AddressType table in the AdventureWorks database on the default instance of SQL Server.

■ PART A: Creating a Snapshot Publication

1.   Open SQL Server Management Studio, and connect to the default instance of SQL Server.

2.   Expand Replication, right-click Local Publications, and click New Publication. This brings you to the New Publication Wizard welcome screen.

3.   Click Next to continue.

4.   On the Publication Database screen, highlight AdventureWorks, and click Next to continue.

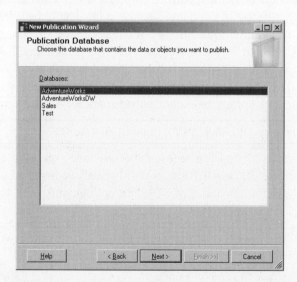

5.   On the Publication Type screen, you can choose what type of publication to create. For this task, choose Snapshot Publication, and click Next to continue.

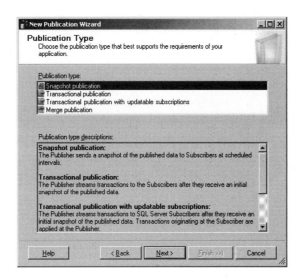

6. On the Articles screen, you can select what data and objects you want to replicate. Expand Tables, and check the AddressType box.

7. You can also set the properties for an article from this screen. Make sure AddressType is highlighted, click Article Properties, and then click Set Properties of Highlighted Table Article.

8. In the Destination Object section, change the destination object name to ReplicatedType, change the destination object owner to dbo, and click OK.

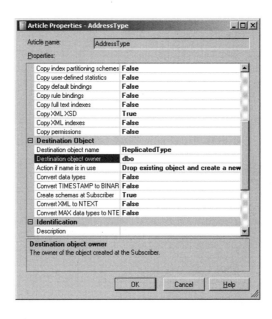

9. Back at the Articles screen, click Next to continue.

10. On the next screen, you can filter the data that is replicated. You do not want to filter the data in this case, so click Next to continue.

11. On the Snapshot Agent screen, check the box to create a snapshot immediately, and check the Schedule the Snapshot agent to run at the following times. Leave the default schedule of one hour, and click Next.

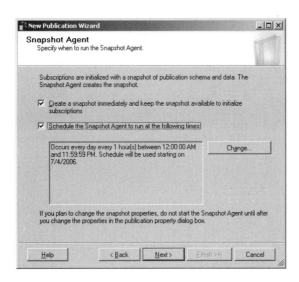

12. On the Agent Security screen, you are asked how the agents should log in and access data. To set this for the snapshot agent, click the Security Settings button next to Snapshot Agent.

13. Ordinarily you would create an account for the agent to run under, but to make the task simpler, you will run the agent using the SQL Server Agent account, so select the radio button for that option, and click OK.

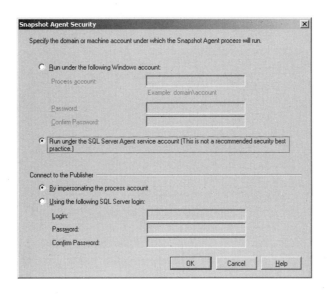

14. Back at the Agent Security screen, click Next to continue.

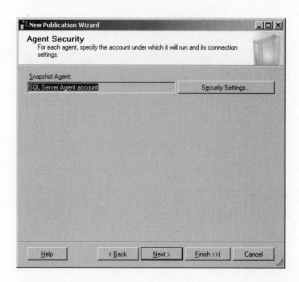

15. On the Wizard Actions screen, you can have the wizard create the publication, write a script to create the publication you can run later, or do both. Leave the Create the Publication box checked, and click Next to continue.

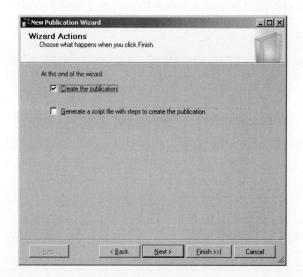

16. On the Complete the Wizard screen, you need to enter a name for the new publication, so enter AddressTypePub, and click Finish.

17. When the wizard is finished, click Close.

Question 3	You have a partial T1 connection and a very large database. Is this an acceptable solution? If you decide no, what are your alternatives while still using a replication scenario?

■ PART B: Verifying Results

1. Open SQL Server Management Studio, connect to your SQL Server, expand Replication, and then expand Local Publications. You should see the AddressTypePub publication listed.

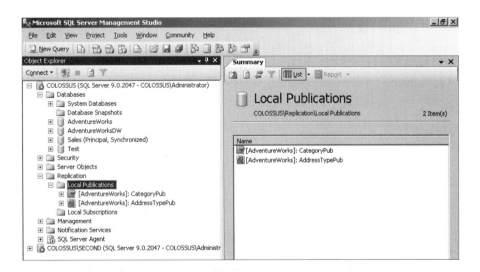

2. Right-click AddressTypePub, and click Properties. The type should be Snapshot.

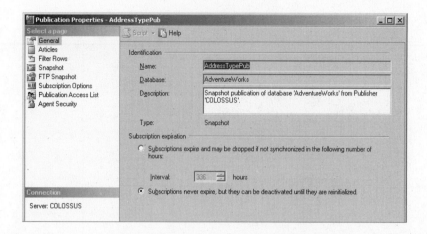

3. Click OK.

Exercise 23.7	Subscribing to a Snapshot Publication
Scenario	You work for a medium-sized company that has offices throughout the world. The sales department in the Tucson branch office needs access to one of the databases housed on the SQL Server at the corporate headquarters. They will use the data for reporting purposes only, so they will not be making updates to their local copy of the data. They need the data to be refreshed only once a day, so you can allow for a full day of latency. They are connected by a partial T1 that is at about 75 percent capacity during peak hours, but off-hours it is at about 30 percent capacity, so the network has plenty of room during off hours. You have already configured a snapshot publication at the headquarters; now you must create a subscription on the server in Tucson.
Duration	This task should take approximately 30 minutes.
Setup	For this task, you need access to the machine you installed SQL Server 2005 on in Exercise 2.1, the Second instance of SQL Server installed in Exercise 2.2, the AdventureWorks database installed with the sample data, the default instance of SQL Server configured as a distributor in Exercise 23.3, and the snapshot publication configured in Exercise 23.6.
Caveat	Make sure the SQL Agent service for the Second instance is set to start automatically before starting this task.
Procedure	In this task, you will create a pull subscription to the snapshot publication on your default instance of SQL Server.
Equipment Used	For this task, you need access to the machine you installed SQL Server 2005 on in Exercise 2.1, the Second instance of SQL Server installed in Exercise 2.2, the AdventureWorks database installed with the sample data, the default instance of SQL Server configured as a distributor in Exercise 23.3, and the snapshot publication configured in Exercise 23.6.
Objective	To create a pull subscription to the snapshot publication on the default instance of SQL Server.
Criteria for Completion	This task is complete when replication is running properly.

■ PART A: Subscribing to a Snapshot Publication

1. Open SQL Server Management Studio, and connect to the Second instance by selecting it from the Server Name drop-down list.

2. Expand Replication, right-click Local Subscriptions, and click New Subscription. This brings you to the New Subscription Wizard welcome screen. Click Next to continue.

3. On the Publication screen, select the default instance of your server from the Publisher drop-down list, select AddressTypePub from the Databases and Publications list, and click Next to continue.

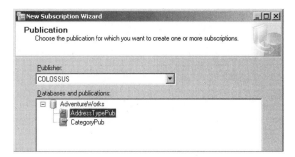

4. On the Distribution Agent Location screen, you are asked which machine should run the replication agents—at the distributor or at the subscriber. Because you want to create a pull subscription, select the Run Each Agent at Its Subscriber option, and click Next.

5. On the Subscribers screen, you can choose a subscriber for the publication. Check the box next to the Second instance of your server.

6. Then the drop-down list is populated with all the available databases on the subscriber. Select New Database from the list to open the New Database dialog box.

7. Enter SR_Test in the Database Name box, click OK, and then click Next.

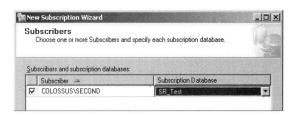

8. On the next screen, you need to set the distribution agent security. To do so, click the ellipsis (…) button in the Subscription Properties list.

9. In a production environment you would create an account for the agent to run under, but to make the task simpler, you will run the agent using the SQL Server Agent account, so select the radio button for that option, and click OK.

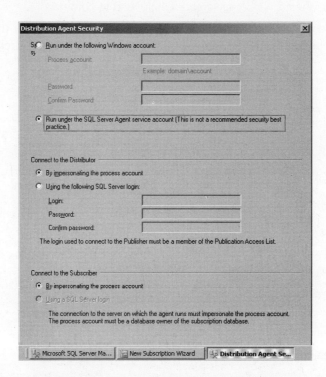

10. Back at the Distribution Agent Security screen, click Next to continue.

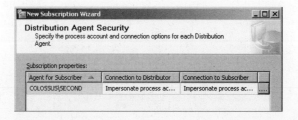

11. The next step is to set the synchronization schedule, so select Define Schedule.

12. In the New Job Schedule dialog box, under Frequency, set Occurs to Daily, and click OK.

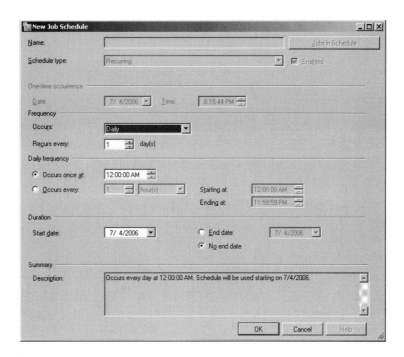

13. Back at the Synchronization Schedule screen, click Next.

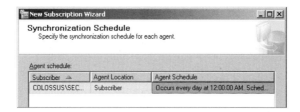

14. On the next screen, you can tell SQL Server when to initialize the subscription, if at all. If you have already created the schema (an empty copy of the database to be replicated) on the subscriber, then you do not need to initialize the subscription. In this case, you should select Immediately from the drop-down list, make sure the Initialize box is checked, and click Next to continue.

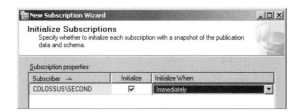

15. On the Wizard Actions screen, you can have the wizard create the subscription, write a script to create the subscription that you can run later, or do both. Leave the Create the Subscription box checked, and click Next to continue.

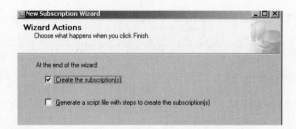

16. On the Complete the Wizard screen, review your options, and click Finish to create the subscription.

17. When the wizard is finished, click Close.

■ PART B: Verifying Results

1. You should have several records in the ReplicatedType table. To verify that, open a new query, connect to the Second instance, and execute the following code:

```
USE SR_Test SELECT * FROM dbo.ReplicatedType
```

2. Now add a new record to the Person.AddressType table in the AdventureWorks database on the default instance. Open a new query, and from the Query menu, select Connection and Change Connection. Then connect to the default instance.

3. Run the following code to add a new record:

```
USE AdventureWorks INSERT INTO Person.AddressType (Name) VALUES ('Tucson
Office')
```

4. Now you could wait for 24 hours or so for this to replicate, but that is a bit too long, so you need to run replication manually. To start, expand your default instance server in Object Explorer.

5. Expand SQL Agent, and then expand Jobs.

6. Right-click the job whose name starts with <YourServerName>-AdventureWorks-AddressType Pub-2, click Start Job at Step, and select Step 1.

7. Click Close when the job is complete.

8. Next, expand your Second instance in Object Explorer.

9. Expand SQL Agent, and then expand Jobs.

10. Right-click the job whose name starts with <YourServerName>-AdventureWorks-AddressType Pub-<YourServerName>\SECOND-SR_Test, and click Start Job at Step.

11. Click Close when the job is complete.

12. Run the following query against the Second instance:

    ```
    USE SR_Test SELECT * FROM dbo.ReplicatedType
    ```

13. One of the records in the result set should be the new Tucson Office record.

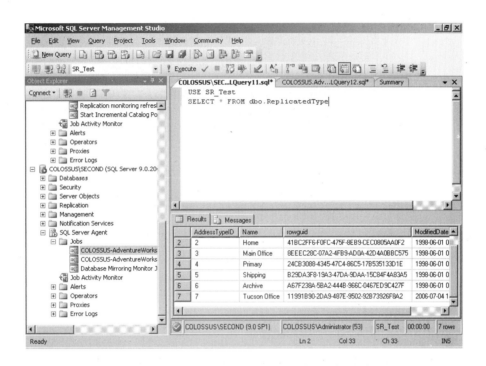

Exercise 23.8	Creating a Merge Publication
Scenario	You work for a medium-sized company that has offices throughout the world. The retail division of your company manages shops in various cities. Each shop maintains its own inventory database. The retail manager in Phoenix wants each of her four shops to be able to share inventory with each other so employees can pick up a part from another nearby store rather than wait for a shipment from the manufacturer. To do this, employees at each shop need to be able to update their local copy of the inventory database, decrement the other store's inventory, and then go pick up the part. This way, the other store won't sell its part because the part will have already been taken out of stock. To accomplish this goal, you have decided to create a merge publication.
Duration	This task should take approximately 30 minutes.
Setup	For this task, you need access to the machine you installed SQL Server 2005 on in Exercise 2.1, the AdventureWorks database installed with the sample data, and the default instance of SQL Server configured as a distributor, as shown in Exercise 23.3.

Caveat	If you still have log shipping enabled on the AdventureWorks database (from Exercise 20.2), you will need to disable it. Here's how: 1. Open SQL Server Management Studio, and connect to the default instance. 2. Expand Databases, right-click AdventureWorks, point to Tasks, and click Ship Transaction Logs. 3. Uncheck the box next to Enable This as a Primary Database in a Log Shipping Configuration. 4. Click Yes in the subsequent dialog box, and then click OK. 5. Click Close when the configuration is complete.
Procedure	In this task, you will create a merge publication on your default instance of SQL Server on the ProductionCulture table in the AdventureWorks database.
Equipment Used	For this task, you need access to the machine you installed SQL Server 2005 on in Exercise 2.1, the AdventureWorks database installed with the sample data, and the default instance of SQL Server you configured as a distributor in Exercise 23.3.
Objective	To create a merge publication.
Criteria for Completion	This task is complete when you have created a merge publication based on the Production.Culture table in the AdventureWorks database on the default instance of SQL Server.

■ PART A: Creating a Merge Publication

1. Open SQL Server Management Studio, and connect to your SQL Server.
2. Expand Replication, right-click Local Publications, and click New Publication. This brings you to the New Publication Wizard welcome screen.
3. Click Next to continue.
4. On the Publication Database screen, highlight AdventureWorks, and click Next to continue.

5. On the Publication Type screen, you can choose what type of publication to create. For this task, choose Merge Publication, and click Next to continue.

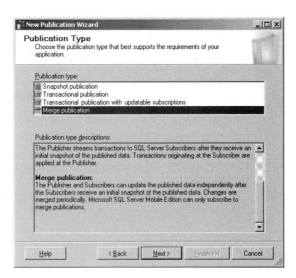

6. On the next screen you are asked what version of SQL Server the subscribers are running. This is because different versions of SQL Server handle merge replication differently. In this case, check only SQL Server 2005, and click Next.

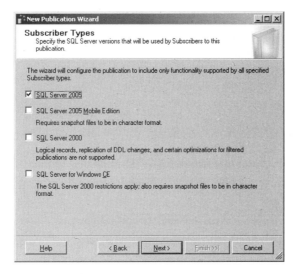

7. On the Articles screen, you can select what data and objects you want to replicate. Expand Tables, and check the Culture box.

8. You can also set the properties for an article from this screen. Make sure Culture is highlighted, click Article Properties, and then click Set Properties of Highlighted Table Article.

9. Notice all of the defaults, but do not make any changes; click OK.

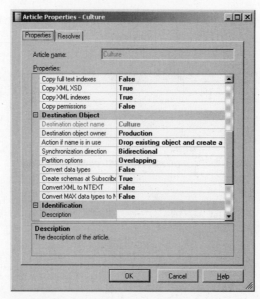

10. Back at the Articles screen, click Next to continue.

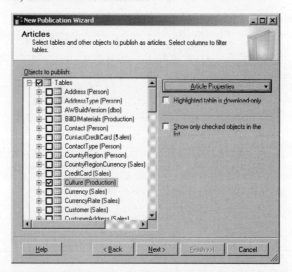

11. On the next screen, you are reminded that a uniqueidentifier column will be added to the replicated table. Click Next to continue.

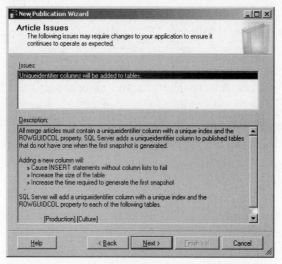

12. On the next screen, you can filter the data that is replicated. You do not want to filter the data in this case, so click Next to continue.

13. On the Snapshot Agent screen, check the box to create a snapshot immediately, and check the Schedule the Snapshot agent to run at the following times. Leave the default schedule, and click Next.

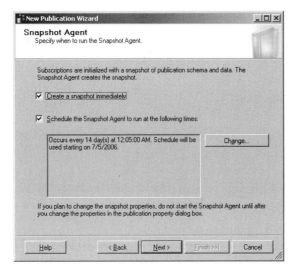

14. On the Agent Security screen, you are asked how the agents should log in and access data. To set this for the snapshot agent, click the Security Settings button next to Snapshot Agent.

15. Ordinarily you would create an account for the agent to run under, but to make the task simpler, you will run the agent using the SQL Server Agent account, so select the radio button for that option, and click OK.

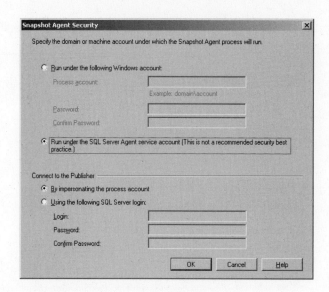

16. Back at the Agent Security screen, click Next to continue.

17. On the Wizard Actions screen, you can have the wizard create the publication, write a script to create the publication that you can run later, or do both. Leave the Create the Publication box checked, and click Next to continue.

18. On the Complete the Wizard screen, you need to enter a name for the new publication, so enter CulturePub, and click Finish.

19. When the wizard is finished, click Close.

■ PART B: Verifying Results

1. Open SQL Server Management Studio, connect to your SQL Server, and expand Replication. You should see the CulturePub publication listed.

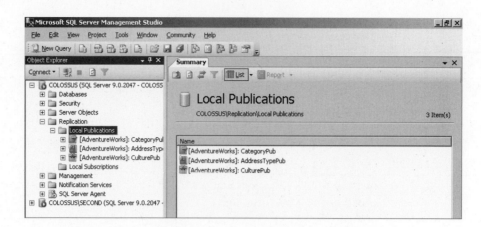

2. Right-click CulturePub, and click Properties. The type should be Merge.

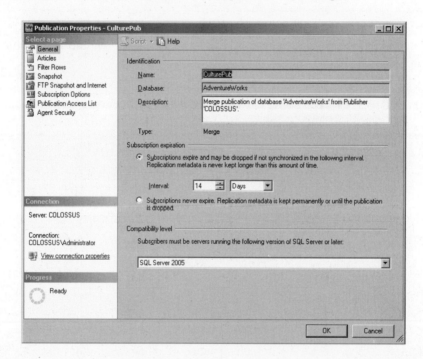

3. Click OK.

Exercise 23.9	Subscribing to a Merge Publication
Scenario	You work for a medium-sized company that has offices throughout the world. The retail division of your company manages shops in various cities. Each shop maintains its own inventory database. The retail manager in Phoenix wants each of her four shops to be able to share inventory with each other so employees can pick up a part from another nearby store rather than wait for a shipment from the manufacturer. To do this, employees at each shop need to be able to update their local copy of the inventory database, decrement the other store's inventory, and then go pick up the part. This way, the other store won't sell its part because the part will have already been taken out of stock. You

	have already configured a merge publication to which you must now subscribe.
Duration	This task should take approximately 30 minutes.
Setup	For this task, you need access to the machine you installed SQL Server 2005 on in Exercise 2.1, the Second instance of SQL Server installed in Exercise 2.2, the AdventureWorks database installed with the sample data, the default instance of SQL Server you configured as a distributor in Exercise 23.3, and the merge publication you configured in Exercise 23.8.
Caveat	Make sure the SQL Agent service for the Second instance is set to start automatically before starting this task.
Procedure	In this task, you will create a pull subscription to the merge publication on your default instance of SQL Server.
Equipment Used	For this task, you need access to the machine you installed SQL Server 2005 on in Exercise 2.1, the Second instance of SQL Server installed in Exercise 2.2, the AdventureWorks database installed with the sample data, the default instance of SQL Server you configured as a distributor in Exercise 23.3, and the merge publication you configured in Exercise 23.8.
Objective	To subscribe to a merge publication.
Criteria for Completion	This task is complete when replication is running properly.

■ PART A: Subscribing to a Merge Publication

1. Open SQL Server Management Studio, and connect to the Second instance by selecting it from the Server Name drop-down list.

2. Expand Replication, right-click Local Subscriptions, and click New Subscription. Click Next to continue. This brings you to the New Subscription Wizard welcome screen.

3. On the Publication screen, select the default instance of your server from the Publisher drop-down list. Select CulturePub from the Databases and Publications list, and click Next to continue.

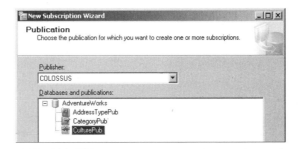

4. On the Merge Agent Location screen, you are asked which machine should run the replication agents—at the distributor or at the subscriber. Because you want to create a pull subscription, select the Run Each Agent at Its Subscriber option, and click Next.

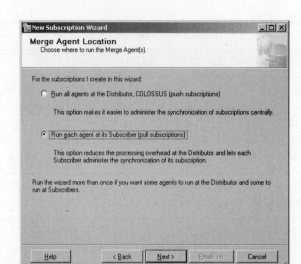

5. On the Subscribers screen, you can choose a subscriber for the publication. Check the box next to your server.

6. Then the drop-down list is populated with all the available databases on the subscriber. Select New Database from the list to open the New Database dialog box.

7. Enter MR_Test in the Database Name box, and click OK. Then click Next.

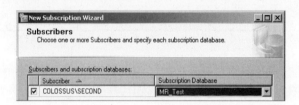

8. On the next screen you need to set the merge agent security. To do so, click the ellipsis (…) button in the Subscription Properties list.

9. Ordinarily you would create an account for the agent to run under, but to make the task simpler, you will run the agent using the SQL Server Agent account, so select the radio button for that option, and click OK.

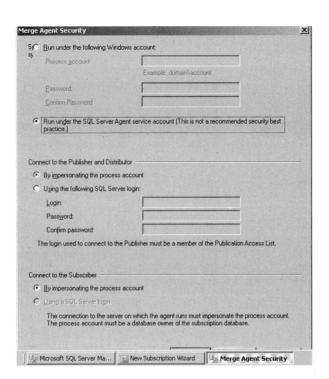

10. Back at the Merge Agent Security screen, click Next to continue.

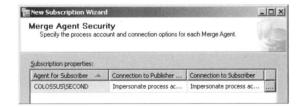

11. The next step is to set the synchronization schedule, so select Define Schedule.

12. In the New Job Schedule dialog box, make these changes:
    - Under Frequency, set Occurs to Daily
    - Under Daily Frequency, select Occurs Every, and set the interval to 10 minutes.

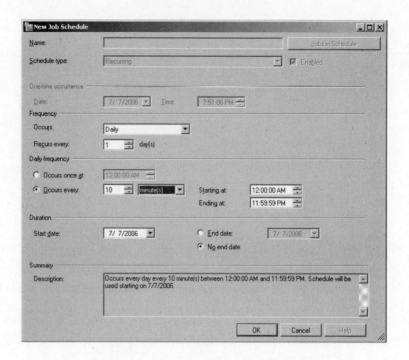

13. Click OK.
14. Back at the Synchronization Schedule screen, click Next.

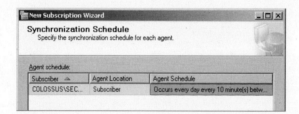

15. On the next screen, you can tell SQL Server when to initialize the subscription, if at all. If you have already created the schema (an empty copy of the database to be replicated) on the subscriber, then you do not need to initialize the subscription. In this case, you should select Immediately from the drop-down list, make sure the Initialize box is checked, and click Next to continue.

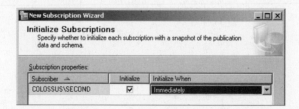

16. The next screen shows you how conflicts will be resolved when they occur. In this case, select the defaults, and click Next.

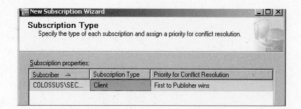

17. On the Wizard Actions screen, you can have the wizard create the subscription, write a script to create the subscription that you can run later, or do both. Leave the Create the Subscription box checked, and click Next to continue.

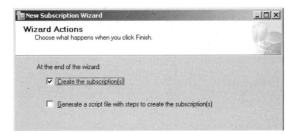

18. On the Complete the Wizard screen, review your options, and click Finish to create the subscription.

19. When the wizard is finished, click Close.

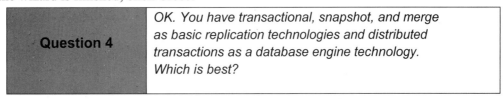

Question 4	OK. You have transactional, snapshot, and merge as basic replication technologies and distributed transactions as a database engine technology. Which is best?

■ PART B: Verifying Results

1. You should have several records in the Culture table. To verify that, open a new query, connect to the Second instance, and execute the following code:

```
USE MR_Test SELECT * FROM Production.Culture
```

2. Now add a new record to the Production.Culture table in the AdventureWorks database on the default instance. Open a new query, and from the Query menu, select Connection and Change Connection. Then connect to the default instance.

3. Run the following code to add a new record:

```
USE AdventureWorks INSERT INTO Production.Culture (CultureID, Name)
VALUES('DE', 'German')
```

4. Wait about 10 minutes, and run the following query against the Second instance:

```
USE MR_Test SELECT * FROM Production.Culture
```

5. One of the records in the result set should be the new DE record.

6. Now to test replication from the subscriber back to the publisher, run the following code on the Second instance to add a new record:

```
USE MR_Test INSERT INTO Production.Culture (CultureID, Name) VALUES('AL',
'Albanian')
```

7. Wait about 10 minutes, and run the following query against the default instance. You should see the new AL record:

```
USE AdventureWorks SELECT * FROM Production.Culture
```

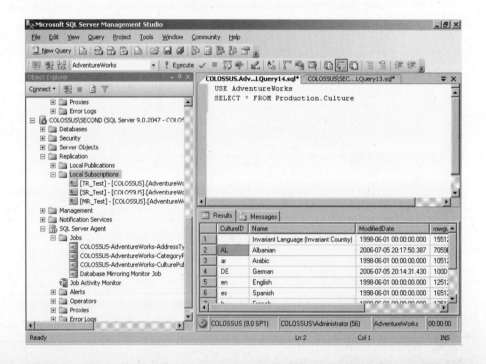

Exercise 23.10	Resolving Merge Conflicts
Scenario	You have created a merge publication and a corresponding subscription so employees at each of the four shops in Phoenix are able to share inventory with each other and automatically affect inventory. This has been working fine for some time, but recently two of the stores tried to get a part from a third store at the same time. This has caused a merge conflict that you need to resolve.
Duration	This task should take approximately 30 minutes.

Setup	For this task, you need access to the machine you installed SQL Server 2005 on in Exercise 2.1, the Second instance of SQL Server installed in Exercise 2.2, the AdventureWorks database installed with the sample data, the default instance of SQL Server you configured as a distributor in Exercise 23.3, the merge publication you configured in Exercise 23.8, and a subscription to the merge publication you configured in Exercise 23.9.
Caveat	This task doesn't have any caveats.
Procedure	In this task, you will create and resolve a merge conflict.
Equipment Used	For this task, you need access to the machine you installed SQL Server 2005 on in Exercise 2.1, the second instance of SQL Server installed in Exercise 2.2, the AdventureWorks database installed with the sample data, the default instance of SQL Server you configured as a distributor in Exercise 23.3, the merge publication you configured in Exercise 23.8, and a subscription to the merge publication you configured in Exercise 23.9.
Objective	To create a merge conflict.
Criteria for Completion	This task is complete when you have successfully created and resolved a conflict in a merge publication.

■ PART A: Resolving Merge Conflicts

1. First you will update a record in the Production.Culture table in the AdventureWorks database on the default instance. Open a new query, and from the Query menu, select Connection and Change Connection. Then connect to the default instance.

2. Run the following code to update an existing record:

```
USE AdventureWorks UPDATE Production.Culture SET [Name] = 'Dutch' WHERE
CultureID = 'DE'
```

3. Now you will update the same record in the Production.Culture table in the MR_Test database on the Second instance. Open a new query, and from the Query menu, and select Connection and Change Connection. Then connect to the Second instance.

4. Run the following code to update an existing record:

```
USE  MR_Test  UPDATE  Production.Culture  SET  [Name]  =  'Danish'  WHERE
CultureID = 'DE'
```

5. Wait about 10 minutes for the updates to apply before moving on to conflict resolution.

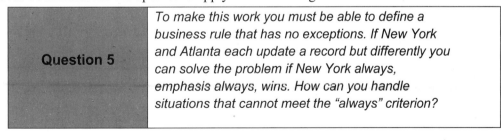

Question 5 — To make this work you must be able to define a business rule that has no exceptions. If New York and Atlanta each update a record but differently you can solve the problem if New York always, emphasis always, wins. How can you handle situations that cannot meet the "always" criterion?

■ PART B: Viewing and Resolving Conflicts

1. In Object Explorer, expand Replication, Publications, right-click the [AdventureWorks]: CulturePub publication, and click View Conflicts.

2. In the Select Conflict Table dialog box, double-click the Culture(1) listing. The (1) denotes that there is one conflict.

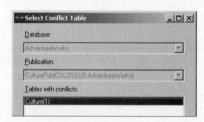

3. In the Replication Conflict Viewer, click the line under Conflict Loser in the top grid. This will change the data on the bottom to show you which record is the winner (currently displayed in all databases) and which is the loser (not shown to anyone).

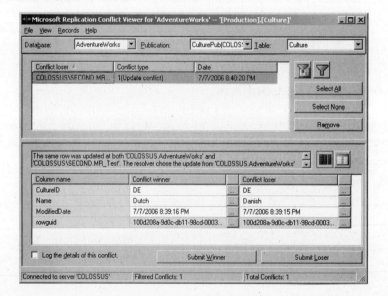

4. Click the Submit Loser button to accept the losing record and discard the winning record (that is, if Dutch is the winner, change it to Danish).

5. Click OK in the subsequent dialog box, and click OK again to exit the Replication Conflict Viewer.

■ PART C: Verifying Results

1. Confirm that there are no more conflicts listed in the dialog box.

Exercise 23.11	Monitoring Replication
Scenario	You have created several publications on your server at corporate headquarters, and you have created several subscriptions on servers throughout your enterprise. Many of these servers are scattered geographically, so it is difficult for you to go there in person to work with the subscriptions. To monitor and configure the publications and subscriptions remotely, you have decided to use Replication Monitor.
Duration	This task should take approximately 15 minutes.
Setup	For this task, you need access to the machine you installed SQL Server 2005 on in Exercise 2.1, the Second instance of SQL Server installed in Exercise 2.2, the AdventureWorks database installed with the sample data, the default instance of SQL Server you configured as a distributor in Exercise 23.3, the transactional publication you configured in Exercise 23.4, and a subscription to the transactional publication you configured in Exercise 23.5.
Caveat	This task doesn't have any caveats.
Procedure	In this task, you will use the Replication Monitor to view replication status. You will insert a tracer record to monitor performance and set up a replication alert.
Equipment Used	For this task, you need access to the machine you installed SQL Server 2005 on in Exercise 2.1, the Second instance of SQL Server installed in Exercise 2.2, the AdventureWorks database installed with the sample data, the default instance of SQL Server you configured as a distributor in Exercise 23.3, the transactional publication you configured in Exercise 23.4, and a subscription to the transactional publication you configured in Exercise 23.5.
Objective	To configure replication properties using the Replication Monitor.
Criteria for Completion	This task is complete when you have successfully viewed and configured replication properties using the Replication Monitor.

■ PART A: Monitoring Replication

1. Open SQL Server Management Studio on the distribution server, which is the default instance.
2. Right-click Replication, and select Launch Replication Monitor.

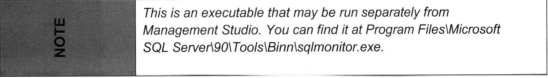

NOTE | *This is an executable that may be run separately from Management Studio. You can find it at Program Files\Microsoft SQL Server\90\Tools\Binn\sqlmonitor.exe.*

3. Expand your server to view the publications available.

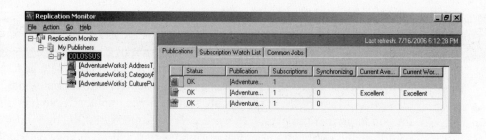

4. Switch to the Subscriptions Watch List tab. From here you can view reports about the performance of all publications and subscriptions that this distributor handles.

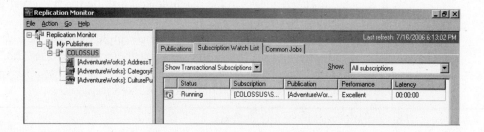

5. Switch to the Common Jobs tab. On this tab, you can view the status of replication jobs that affect all publications and subscriptions handled by this distributor.

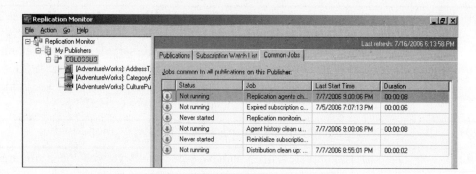

6. Select the CategoryPub publication in the left pane.
7. On the All Subscriptions tab, you can view reports about all the subscriptions for this particular publication.

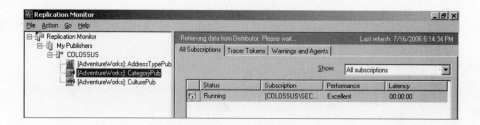

8. Switch to the Tracer Tokens tab. From here you can insert a special record called a tracer token that is used to measure performance for this subscription.
9. To test it, click the Insert Tracer button, and wait for the results.

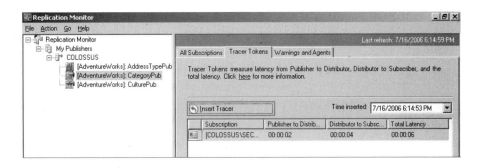

10. Switch to the Warnings and Agents tab. From here you can change settings for agents and configure replication alerts.

11. Click the Configure Alerts button, select Replication: Agent Failure, and click Configure.

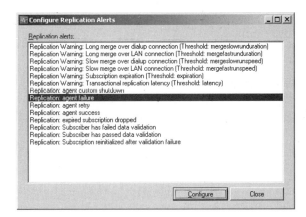

12. Notice that this opens a new alert dialog box. Check the Enable box, and click OK to enable this alert.

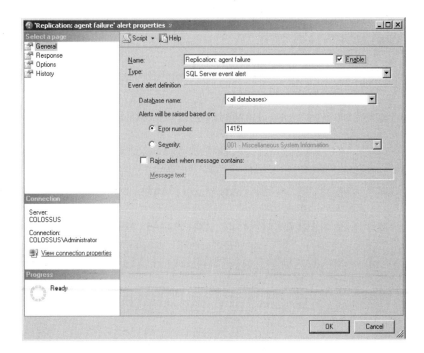

13. Click Close to return to Replication Monitor.

14. Close Replication Monitor.

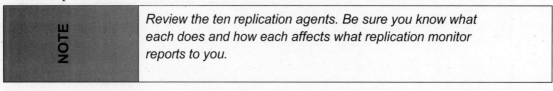

> **NOTE** *Review the ten replication agents. Be sure you know what each does and how each affects what replication monitor reports to you.*

■ PART B: Verifying Results

1. Open SQL Server Management Studio on the distribution server, which is the default instance.

2. In Object Explorer, expand your server, and then expand SQL Server Agent.

3. Click Alerts, and you should see the Replication: Agent Failure alert in the right pane.

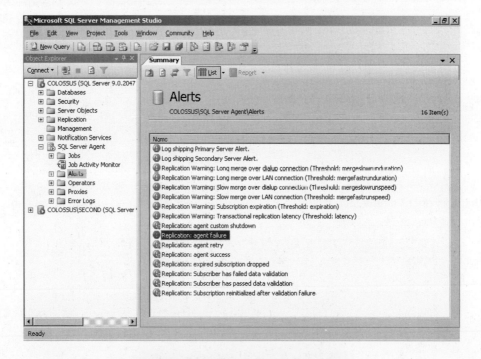

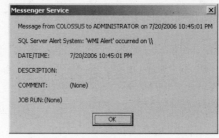